CREATIVE BIBLE ACTIVITIES FOR CHILDREN
by
SARAH LIU
and
MARY LOU VITTITOW

VICTOR BOOKS a division of SP Publications, Inc.
WHEATON, ILLINOIS 60187

Offices also in
Whitby, Ontario, Canada
Amersham-on-the-Hill, Bucks, England

Illustrated by Mary Lou Vittitow

Sixth printing, 1984

Library of Congress Catalog Card Number: 77-80440

ISBN: 0-88207-466-0

Printed in the United States of America

VICTOR BOOKS
A division of SP Publications, Inc.
Wheaton, Ill. 60187

ABOUT THIS BOOK . . .

Our goal in developing the activities in this book is to make learning the Bible an exciting and fun experience. We have selected some of the outstanding stories of the Bible on which we have based all the activities. However, most games, art projects, and activity sheets can be adapted to any lesson being taught. For example, the "Hang It Right" game on pages 11 and 12 for "Creation" can be used for any story requiring sequence just by changing the pictures. For older children, facts could be substituted for pictures, but the same basic board can still be used.

Also, the games are designed to be carried around easily. Each child selects the game to meet his own needs and takes it to a quiet corner to play and learn. Since most of the games are self-checking, the teacher is free to observe and give assistance when needed.

Like the games, the art projects are adaptable. For instance, the whale mobile included in "Creation" could also be used for the story of "Jonah." We have provided patterns for some of the art activities for young children. However, older children can draw their own patterns.

Where the art project is not suitable for both younger and older children, we have provided two art projects. All of these projects have actually been made by children in classroom situations. Where one project is listed for two age groups, the authors have found, through experience, that it is successful with both groups.

Three activity sheets at different levels of difficulty are provided for each topic. We have attempted to design them in such a way that children of all ages will have fun while learning. Again, the ideas used for the activities may be applied to many different lessons. For example, the puzzle sheet on page 38 for "Cain and Abel" can be used as a pattern, substituting names and facts from any other Bible story.

Bible references from the King James Version are given on many activity sheets so students can work independently. Answers to the activity sheets are provided at the back of the book. These may be copied on cards and made available to the students if self-checking is desired.

All games, puzzles, and activities in this book are based on the King James Version of the Bible.

The coding used in the Table of Contents for suggested age levels is as follows:

A - 4-5 years
B - 6-8 years
C - 9-11 years

These age levels indicated for the games, art projects, and activity sheets are meant only as a guide, and teacher judgment will determine which activities are most suitable for each group of children.

"Love suffereth long . . . beareth all things, believeth all things, hopeth all things, endureth all things . . ." This has been true of our families to whom we dedicate this book.

Allen
Chet
Julie

Mary Lou Vittitow

Kenneth
Sharene

Sarah Liu

Helpful Hints

Listed below are a few ideas that have proved helpful to us:

1. It is helpful to the children if all parts of a game are kept together with the gameboard. The authors have purchased zippered plastic bags that have served this purpose well.

2. Games need to be attractive (use lots of contrasting colors) as well as durable. We suggest laminating all the games and their parts. However, if laminating film is not available, clear contact paper makes a good substitute.

3. After a game is laminated or covered with contact paper, only permanent felt markers will write on it. Two brands we have had success with are:

   Broad tip: El Marko permanent marker by Flair
   Thin point: Sanford's Sharpie

4. Games that are made attractively should be displayed where they catch the attention of the children. We suggest game racks similar to the display shelves found in card shops, grocery stores, etc.

5. Don't let a lack of artistic ability discourage you from trying these activities. Parents may be able to help. Or you might enlist the help of other teachers and then share the end products.

6. An opaque projector would be helpful for enlarging the drawings. If you have an overhead projector, transparencies can be made of some items and projected on a large piece of tagboard or construction paper hung on the wall.

7. Old gameboards can often be adapted for many of these games. The children are usually very happy to contribute them.

8. You will be able to find all of the supplies mentioned in this book at school supply houses.

TABLE OF CONTENTS

A - 4-5 years   B - 6-8 years   C - 9-11 years

SUBJECT:	CREATION
BIBLE REFERENCES:	Genesis 1:1-2:14
LEARNING GAME:	Hang It Right
Materials:	Pictures pertaining to Creation story, paper clips, poster board or manila folder, felt pens, ruler
Construction:	Cut pictures for Creation story. Mount on 2" x 3" tagboard cards. On a 10" x 14" poster board draw 2½" x 3½" rectangles to represent frames. Punch holes about 1" from top of each frame. Twist paper clip to make hook. Poke through hole. Put numerals in corner of each frame to show the order in which the pictures go. Cover back of board with contact paper to hide paper clips.
DIRECTIONS FOR PLAYING:	The child puts the pictures in sequential order and can tell the story to a classmate.

1
2
3
4
5
6

SUBJECT: CREATION

ART ACTIVITY: Paper-folded tulip

MATERIALS: Squares of paper suitable for origami (there is a special type of paper sold for this purpose or wrapping paper may be used), green construction paper for stems and leaves, light blue construction paper for background, scissors, glue

TEACHER PREPARATION: Cut paper to be folded into 6" squares.

DIRECTIONS: See illustrated step-by-step directions.

1. Fold a square of paper diagonally.

2. Fold right corner as shown.

3. Fold left corner over.

4. Fold corners toward back as indicated.

5. Make stems and leaves of green construction paper and glue tulip down on background paper.

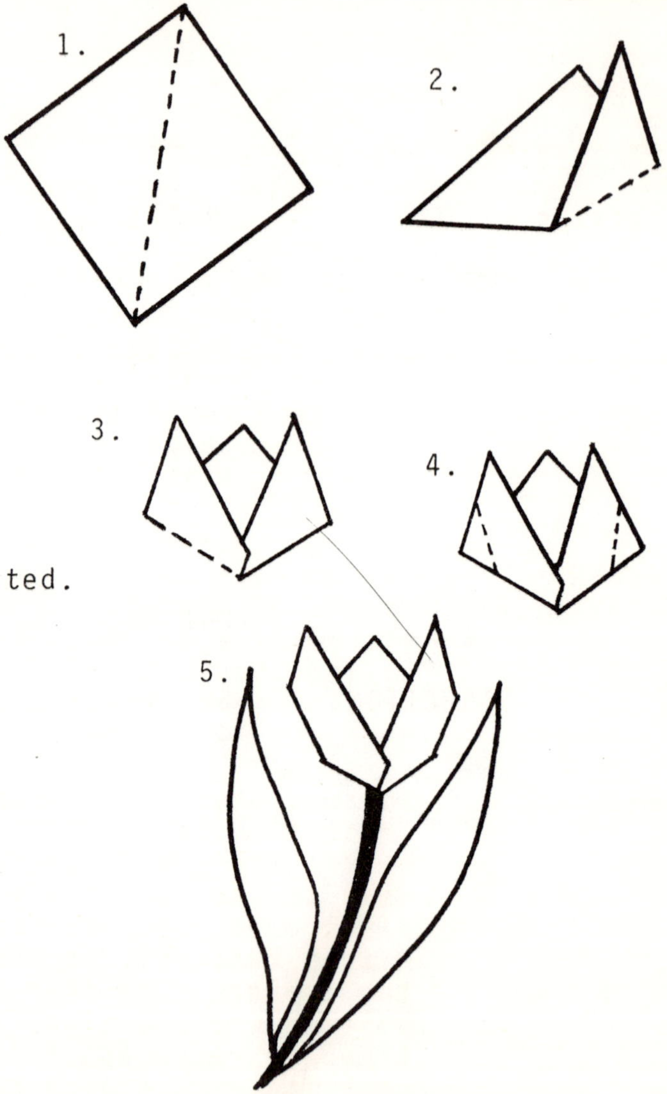

SUBJECT: CREATION

ART ACTIVITY: Popcorn tree

MATERIALS: Brown, orange, pink and green powdered tempera; a teaspoon; and for each child provide:

1 cup popped, unsalted, unbuttered popcorn in a quart plastic bag
1 sheet light blue 9" x 12" construction paper
1 piece 2" x 6" brown construction paper
1 paper plate
Glue
Scissors

TEACHER PREPARATION: Assign each child a season to work on, then put 2 teaspoons of powdered tempera of the appropriate color in his plastic bag with the popcorn. Those working on spring should have pink; those working on summer, green; half of those working on fall, brown; and the other half orange.

DIRECTIONS: The children trim their brown construction paper to represent a tree trunk. For younger children, you may wish to cut the tree trunks. The student then glues the trunk near the bottom of his background paper. Holding the plastic bag securely at the top (or they may be fastened with a twister), he shakes it to coat the popcorn with the tempera. He then empties the colored popcorn on his paper plate and glues it, piece by piece, onto his tree trunk to represent foliage. Those working on fall should work in pairs gluing part orange and part brown "leaves" on their tree. Those working on winter can use the plain white popcorn.

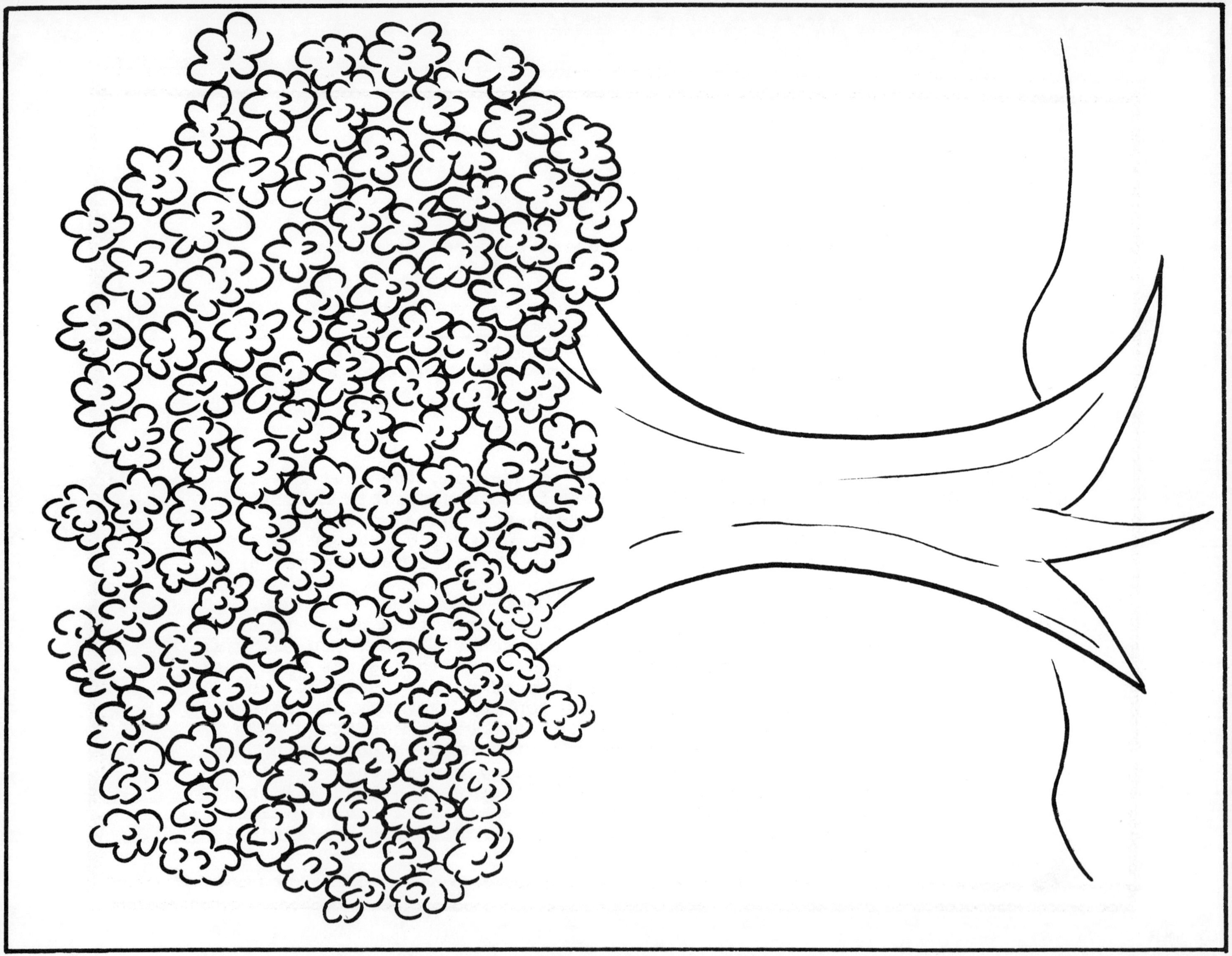

SUBJECT: CREATION

ART ACTIVITY: Whale mobile

MATERIALS: Construction paper, scissors, glue, yarn

TEACHER PREPARATION: For each child, provide the following:

2 pieces 8" x 11" colored construction paper
2 pieces 3" x 2" construction paper of a contrasting color to the above
2 pieces 1" x 1" black construction paper
Yarn for hanging the mobile, approximately 20"

DIRECTIONS: A pattern can be made for each child (see illustration), if desired. The child cuts two whales (as large as possible) from the two 8" x 11" sheets. A large circle is then cut in the middle of both pieces of paper. Holding the 3" x 2" pieces together, cut them into a fish shape. Cut eyes for whale and fish and glue in place. Place yarn between the two pieces of small fish, and glue the two pieces together. Place this fish in the center of the cut-out circle of the whale, leaving enough yarn so it will hang in the center. Glue yarn between the two whale pieces and glue the pieces together.

SUBJECT:	CREATION
ART ACTIVITY:	Underwater scene
MATERIALS:	Background material (this may be craftpaper, large sheet of corrugated cardboard painted blue, or blue plastic cleaning bags). Colored craftpaper or construction paper in colors contrasting to background Lightweight sponge or bubble paper (often used in packing) Shells, coral, etc. (optional) Scissors Glue
TEACHER PREPARATION:	Assemble needed materials and attach background to a bulletin board or wall. Students may be divided into groups or work individually on parts of the scene.
DIRECTIONS:	Draw and cut underwater vegetation and attach to background. Make paper-folded fish and turtle (see directions) and attach. Trim with shells, coral, etc.

TURTLE

1. Start with square of paper. Fold each corner toward center as indicated.

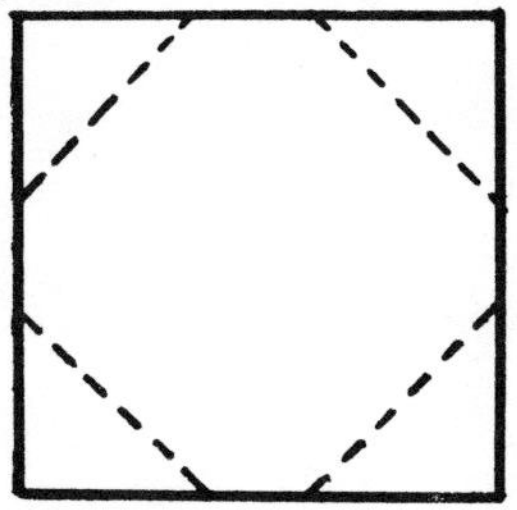

2. For legs, fold rectangle of paper in half lengthwise and trim as shown.

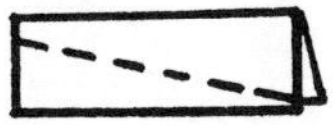

Fold as indicated.

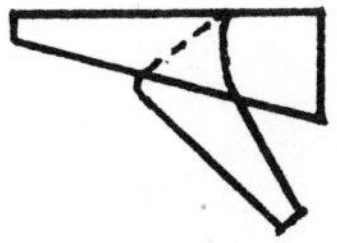

3. For head, fold a small square of paper as shown. Make tail out of scraps.

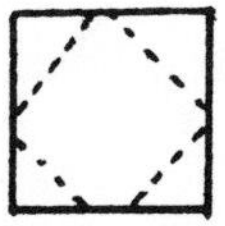

4. Glue head and feet to back of body, making sure folded side is toward you on all pieces. Glue turtle to picture and decorate with cut paper or crayons.

FISH 1

1. Fold square of paper into quarters.

2. Cut small square out of center corner and trim center as shown on diagram.

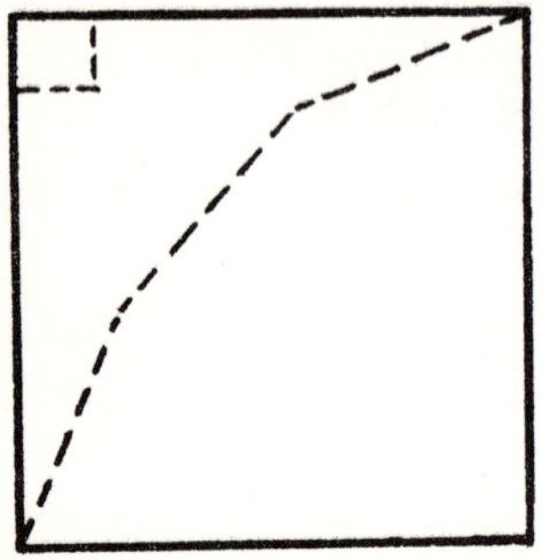

3. Cut diamond-shaped piece out of 2 thicknesses of scraps. Fringe one end of diamond.

4. Glue diamond in place for tail. Glue body in place. Decorate with cut paper or crayons.

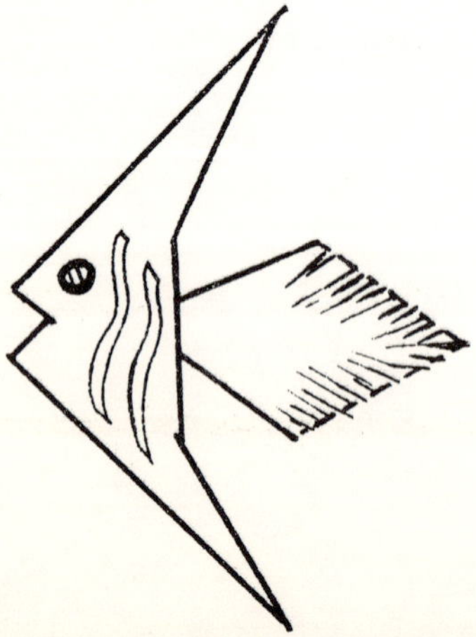

FISH 2

1. Start with square of paper. Fold each corner toward the center as shown.

2. Fold bottom and right tip over toward center. Cut v shape out of left tip.

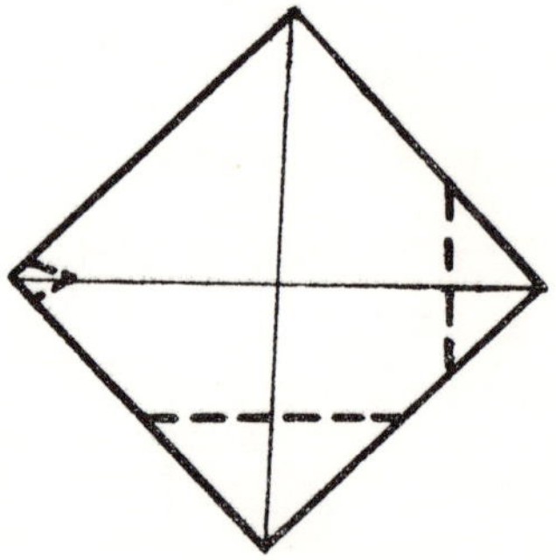

3. Cut and fringe scraps for fins. Glue fins in place. Glue body over fins with folds down. Decorate with cut paper or crayons.

SUBJECT: CREATION

ART ACTIVITY: Cut and paste giraffe

MATERIALS: Brown and yellow construction paper, construction paper of a contrasting color for background

TEACHER PREPARATION: For each child provide the following:

4 strips of brown construction paper 4½" x 3/4"
1 piece brown construction paper 4½" x 3"
1 strip brown construction paper 6" x 1¼"
1 piece brown construction paper 2¼" x 1½"
8 pieces yellow construction paper 1" square

DIRECTIONS: Round off corners of the 4½" x 3" for the body and the 2¼" x 1½" piece for the head. Round off one end of each of the 4½" x 3/4" pieces. Rounding off the corners of the yellow pieces is optional. Cut a tail and an ear from a brown scrap, and an eye from a yellow scrap. Each child should place the pieces before he glues them on the background. The child can use crayons to color in the background.

NOT ACTUAL SIZE

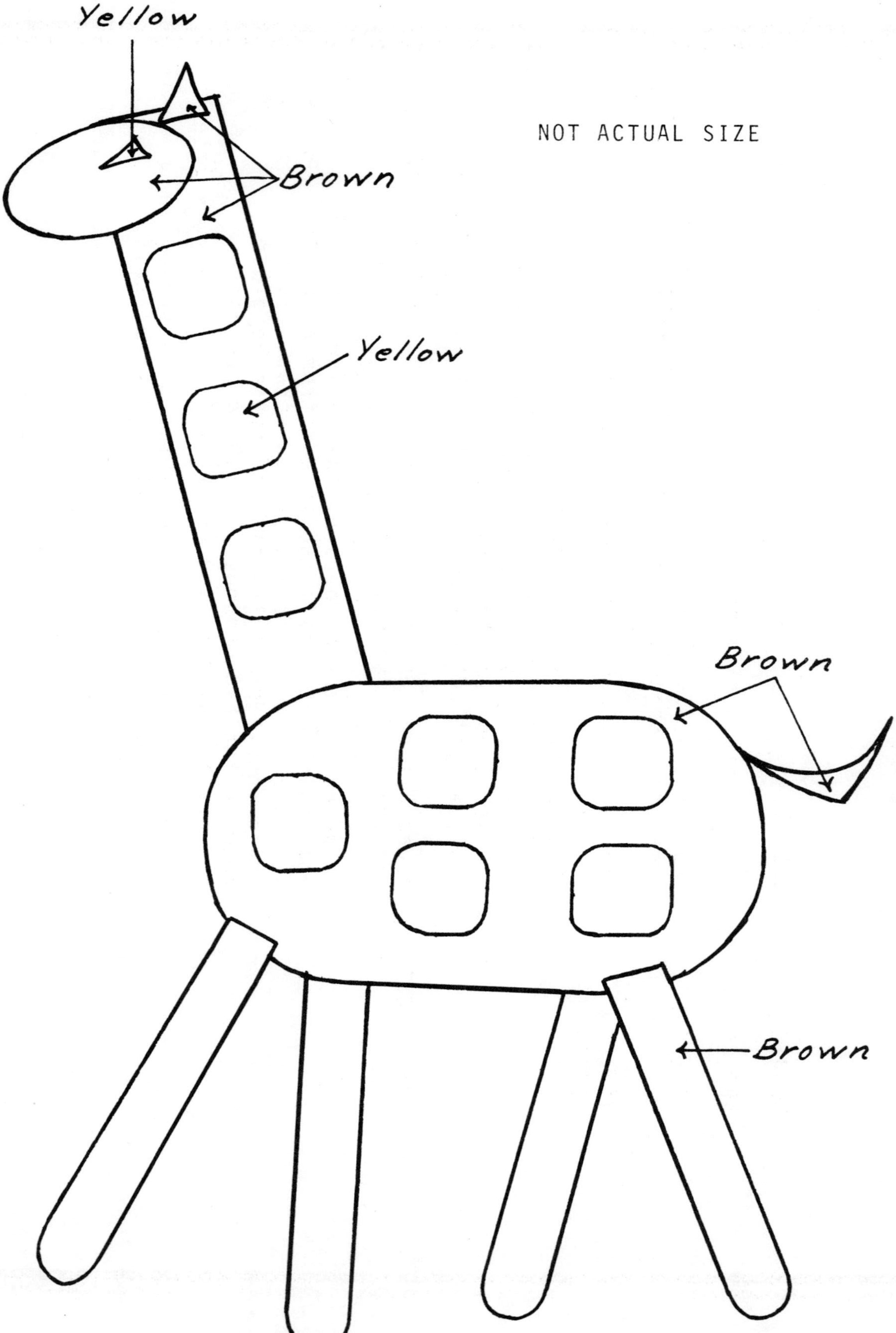

SUBJECT: CREATION

ART ACTIVITY: Self and shadow

MATERIALS: Large sheets of black construction paper, construction paper of a contrasting color, white construction paper, glue, scissors, crayons

TEACHER PREPARATION: Each child needs a sheet of black paper 8½" x 17½", one white and one black piece of paper 5" x 6", and one piece of contrasting paper 6" x 15". If working with younger children, ditto a pattern for each child on a piece of white construction paper 5" x 6". Older children can draw pictures of themselves on the 5" x 6" white construction paper instead of using the ditto.

DIRECTIONS: Fold 6" x 15" paper in half. Unfold. Center it on the black 8½" x 17½" paper and paste down.

Holding the black and white 5" x 6" pieces together, cut outline of self and shadow. Color in picture of self (white piece). Paste self on one half of 6" x 15" contrasting paper with feet touching crease made by fold. Glue shadow on other half with feet touching feet of self.

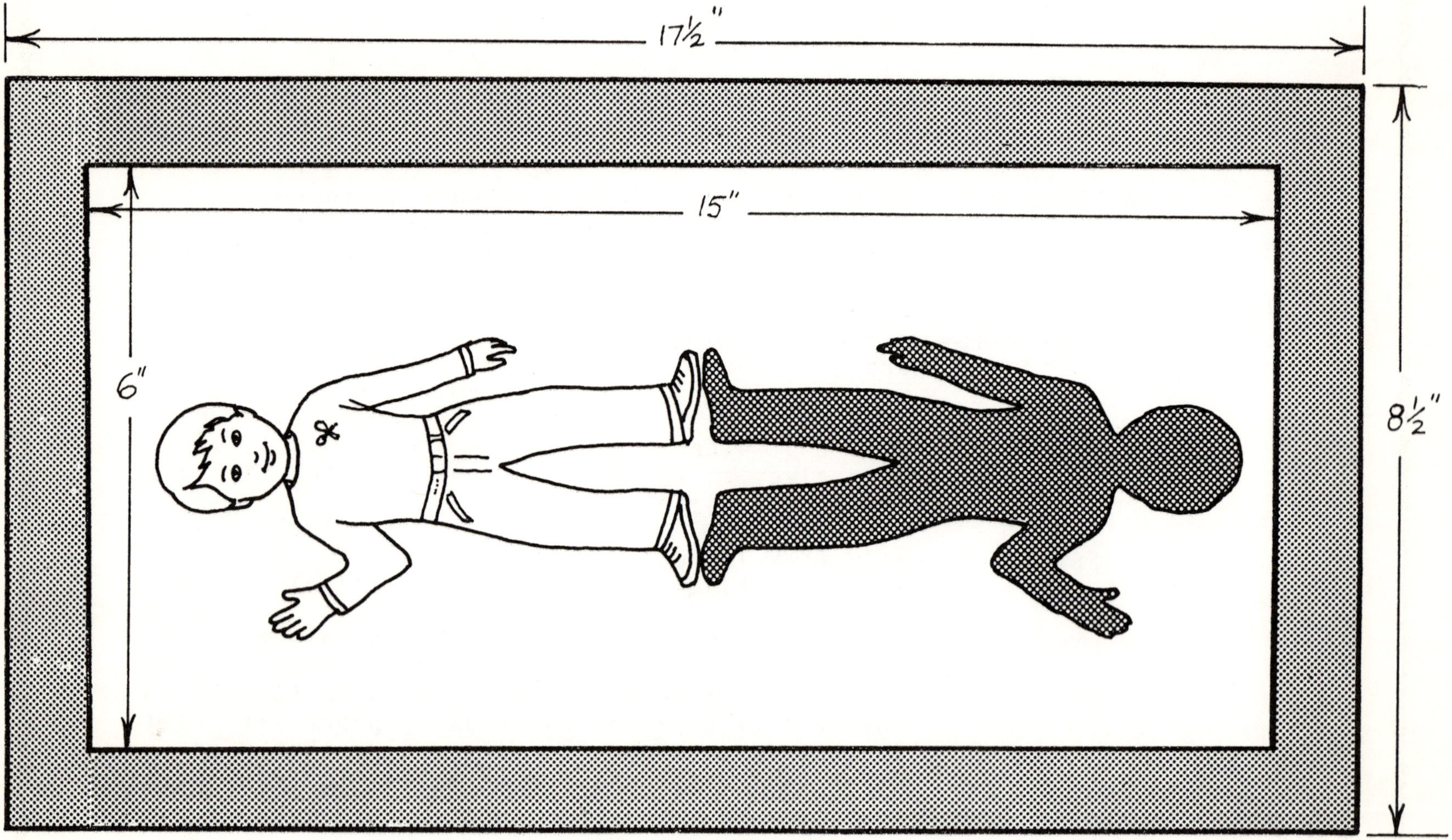
17½"
15"
6"
8½"

COLOR- CUT APART - MATCH THE HALVES

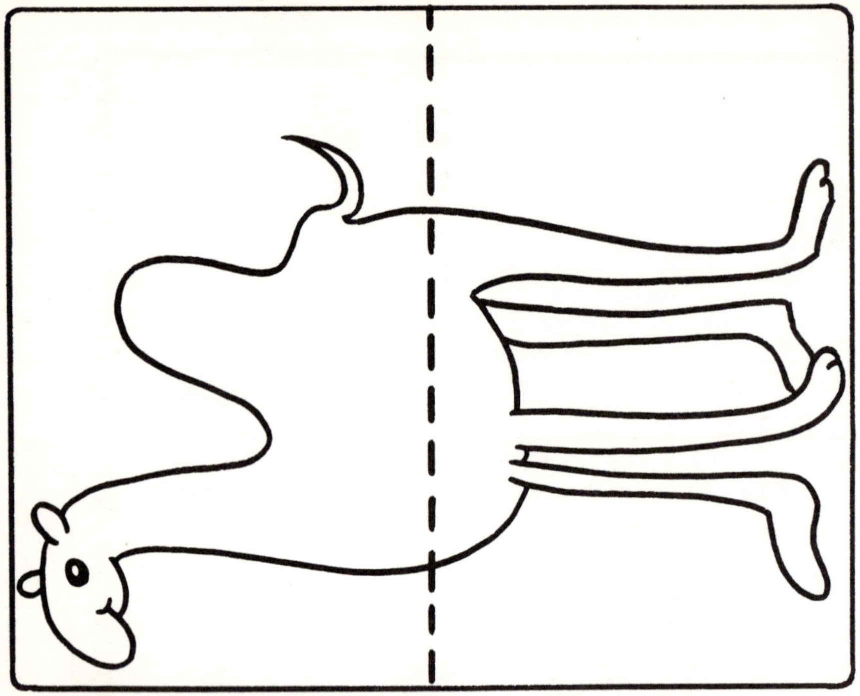

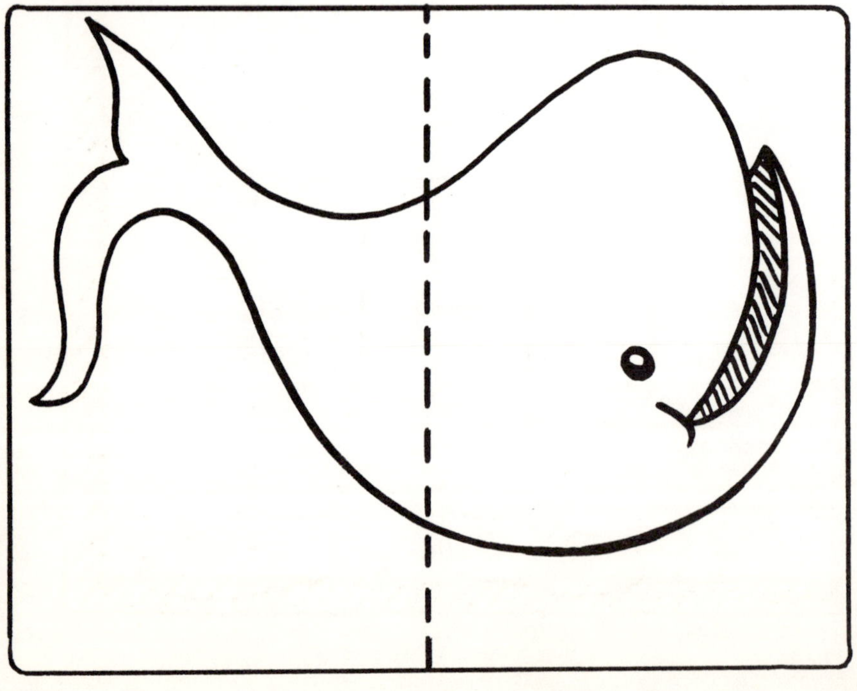

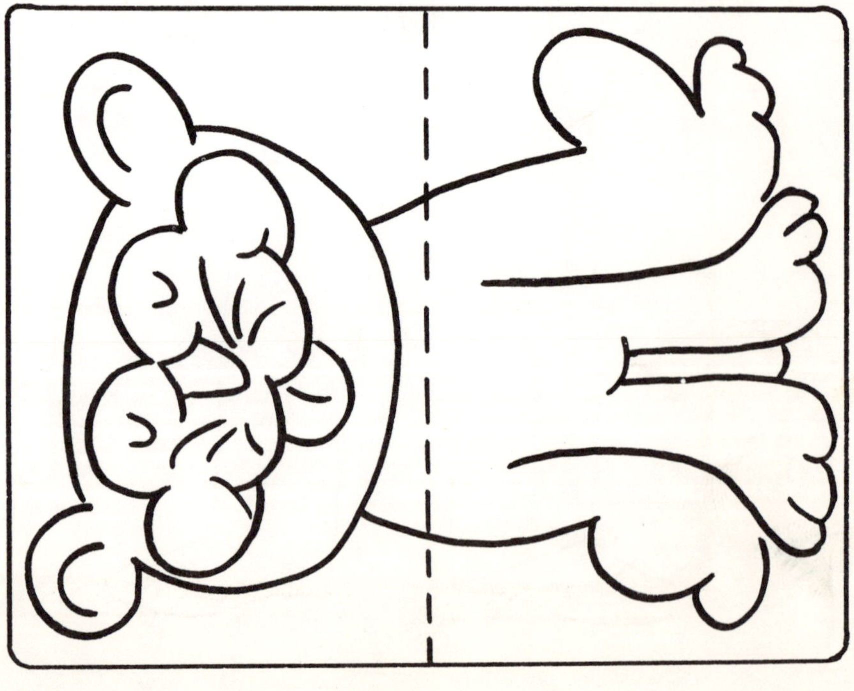

Do you know the story of CREATION? If you do, you can solve this puzzle with the help of the clues given below.

1. Animal with a hump
2. These were created the third day.
3. First woman
4. First man
5. These were created the fourth day.
6. Created the first day
7. Created on the fifth day.
8. God rested on this day.

Read the story of creation in Genesis 1. Then fill in the missing consonants. It is not an exact quotation.

I__ the be__i__ __i__ __ Go__ ma__e the
wo__ __ __. Go__ sai__, " Le__ t __e__e __e
li__ __ __." __e ca__ __ e __ the li__ __ __ Da__,
a__ __ the da__ __ __e__ __ Ni__ __ __. T __i__
wa__ the fi__ __ __ da__.

O__ the se__o__ __ da__, Go__ ma__e
hea__e__.

O__ the t __i__ __ da__, Go__ ma__e the
g__a__ __, t__ee__, a__ __ f__o__e__ __.

O__ the fou__ __ __ da__, __e ma__e the su__,
moo__, a__ __ s__a__ __.

Ne__ __, Go__ c __ea__e__ the fi__ __ a__ __
bi__ __ __.

Fill in the missing consonants: Page 2

O__ the si__ __ __ __ay, Go__ sai__,

" Le__ the ea__ __ __ b__i__ __ fo__ __ __

li__i__ __ c__ea__u__e__."

Bu__ Go__ wa__ lo__e__ __. A__ __ __o

Go__ ma__e ma__.

SUBJECT:	CAIN AND ABEL
BIBLE REFERENCES:	Genesis 4
LEARNING GAME:	Piecing the Puzzle
Materials:	Tagboard, scissors, marker pens
Construction:	Make several copies of each fruit on tagboard. Write word or phrase pertaining to the story on top half of fruit and matching word or phrase on bottom of fruit. For example, write "Cain" on top, and "farmer" on bottom. Cut all fruits in 2 pieces (jigsaw fashion) making sure no two are cut exactly alike.
DIRECTIONS FOR PLAYING:	Child matches the items by fitting the right pieces together.

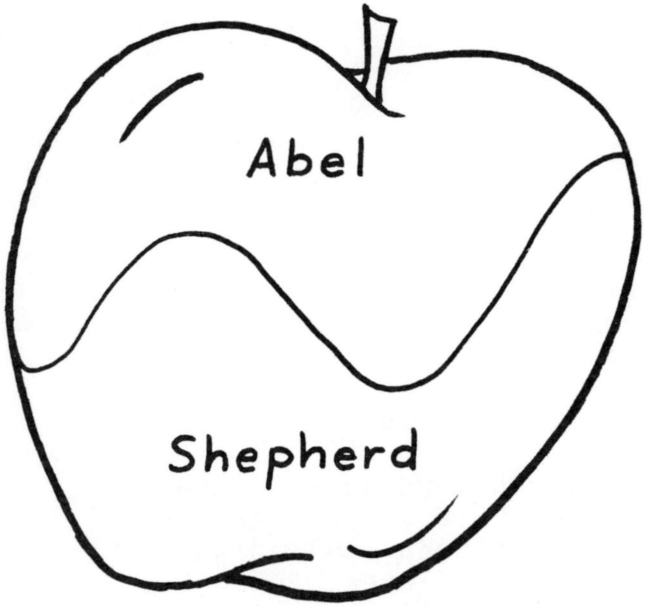
Abel
Shepherd

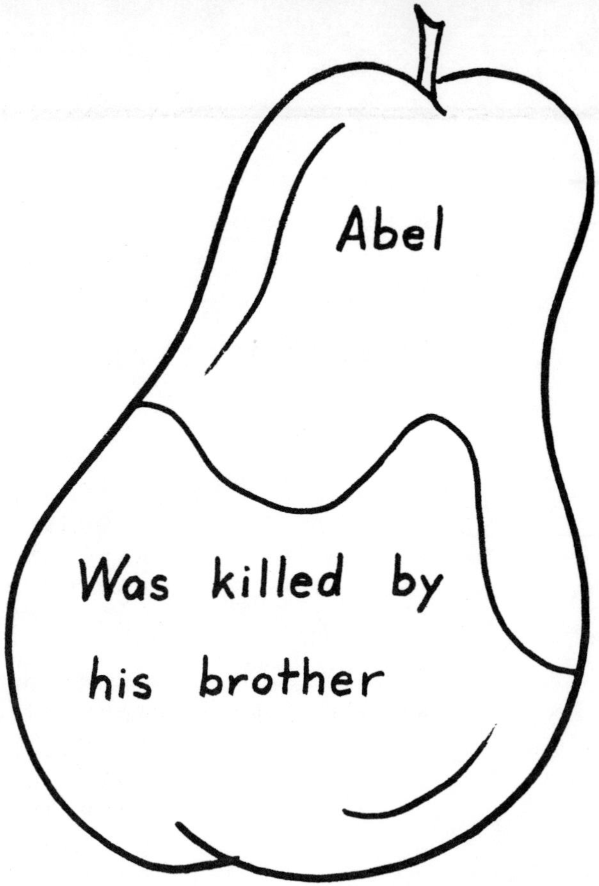
Abel
Was killed by his brother

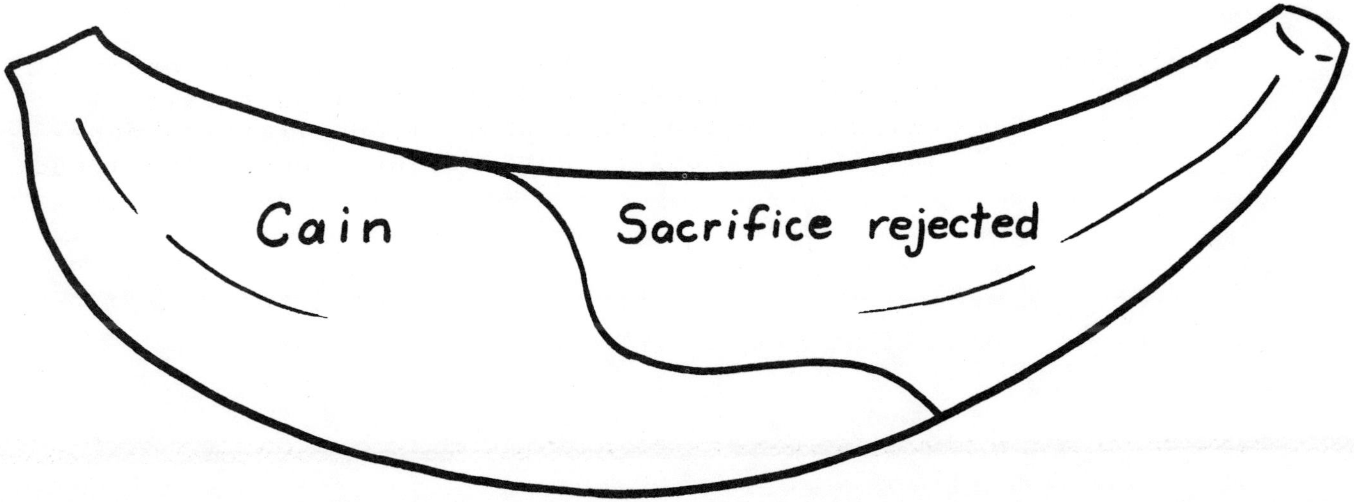
Cain
Sacrifice rejected

SUBJECT:	CAIN AND ABEL
ART ACTIVITY:	Fluffy lamb
MATERIALS:	For each child: White paper--lightweight cardboard or heavy construction paper Lux flakes (or other soap or detergent powder or flakes) Construction paper for background
TEACHER PREPARATION:	Cover working surface with newspaper. Give each child a white paper with a lamb traced on it (see pattern, older children could draw their own). Mix 2 cups Lux Flakes with ½ cup water and beat with electric mixer until it is about the consistency of thick, whipped cream. This will be enough for about 15 children.
DIRECTIONS:	The child cuts out the lamb and glues it on background paper, then dips his fingers into whipped mixture and dabs fluff on lamb to represent fur. About 2 hours drying time is required.

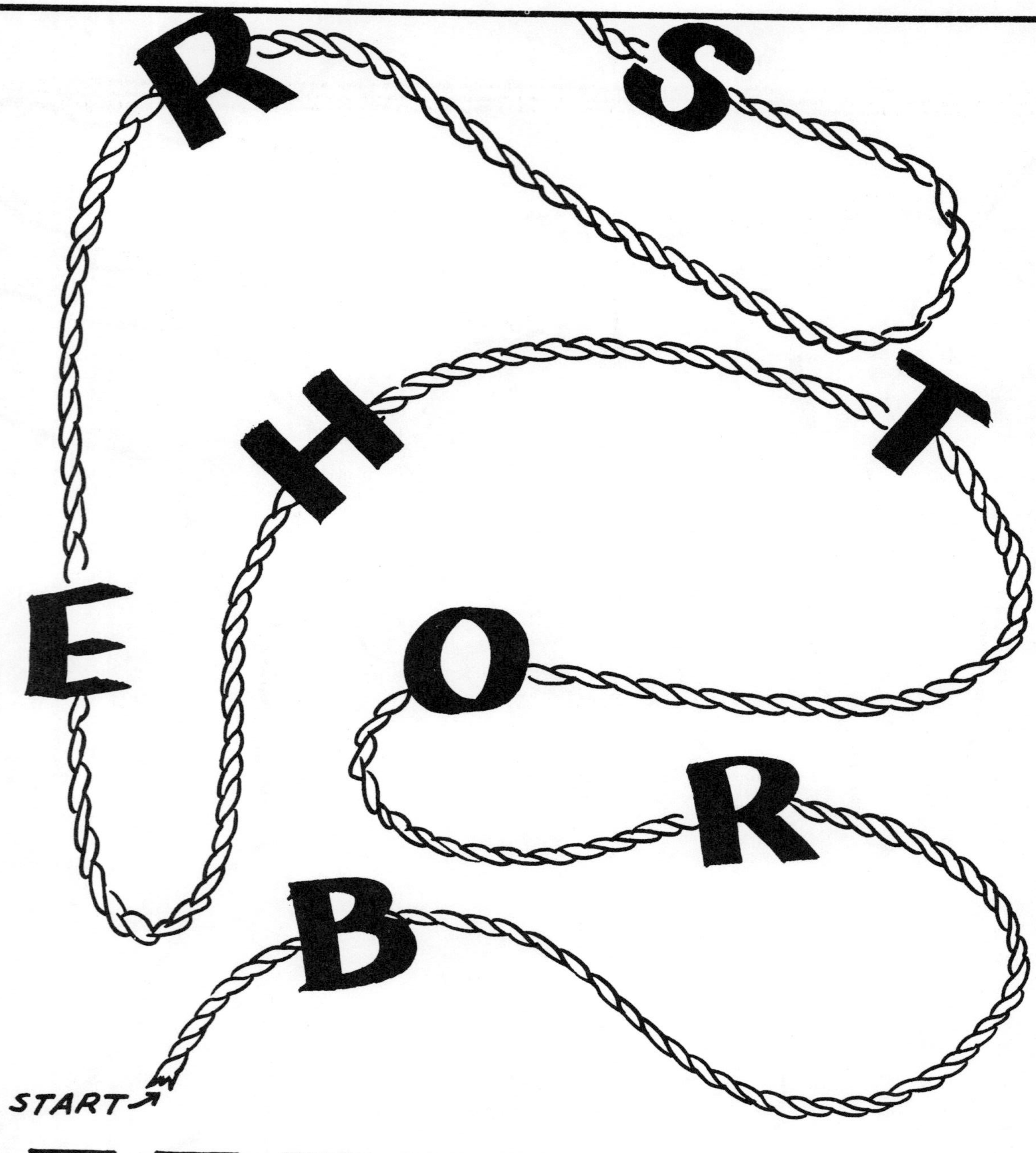

__ __ __ __ __ __ __ __

Follow the rope to find the letters. Write each letter on a line above. The word you find will tell you what Cain and Abel were.

See if you can find 12 words in this puzzle that relate to the story of Cain and Abel. Go up, down, sideways, or diagonally!

S	H	E	P	H	E	R	D
A	D	A	M	A	V	E	E
C	B	T	L	N	E	H	T
R	S	E	L	E	O	T	C
I	D	M	L	D	A	O	E
F	A	R	M	E	R	R	J
I	K	A	S	T	E	B	E
C	A	I	N	S	U	R	R
E	V	I	L	A	R	U	T

Shepherd

Sacrifice

Rejected

Cain

Abel

Farmer

Brother

Evil

Eve

Adam

Tree

Eden

To solve these puzzles, first arrange the letters of the word in the column at the left in alphabetical order. Then, place the rearranged letters in a row (see figure 2). Beneath each of these letters, list in a column the group of letters found beside each letter in the original puzzle. (Be sure to keep the letters in the same order.) When finished, find the message by reading across and separating the words in the correct places.

Example: Fig. 1

C	E	L	I	O	R
A	H	L	H	R	E
I	K	E	S	T	
N	I	D	B	H	

Fig. 2

A	C	I	N
H	E	K	I
L	L	E	D
H	I	S	B
R	O	T	H
E	R		

H e k i l l e d h i s b r o t h e r.

Now you do some!

1.

E	H	S	O	A
N	S	H	O	N
O	W	E	F	
C	T	A	S	C
H	I	T	N	I

_ _ _ _ _ _ _ _ _ _ _ _ _ _ _

_ _ _ _.

2.

L	A	A	V	B	A	U	I
O	D	I	A	O	N	G	V
R	E	N	G	N	D	I	E
D	M	C	A	A	D	F	T

_ _ _ _ _ _ _ _ _ _ _ _ _ _ _ _ _ _

_ _ _ _ _ _ _ _ _ _ _ _ _.

3.

S	I	D	S	I	O	R
L	A	I	I	H	R	E
E	C	D	H	O	B	H
W	N	T	T	S	T	

_ _ _ _ _ _ _ _ _ _ _ _ _ _ _ _

_ _ _ _ _ _ _ _.

SUBJECT:	NOAH
BIBLE REFERENCES:	Genesis 6:1-9:17
LEARNING GAME:	Knowing Noah
Materials:	Tagboard, crayons, construction paper, magnetic strips, glue, marking pen
Construction:	Cut an ark of colored construction paper, drawing details on with marking pen. In each window glue a small magnetic strip. Make 16 tagboard cards the same size as ark windows. On the front of each of 10 cards, write a fact pertaining to Noah. On each of the other six cards write an irrelevant fact. Glue a small magnetic strip on the back of each card.
DIRECTIONS FOR PLAYING:	The child identifies the relevant facts and places them in the ark windows.

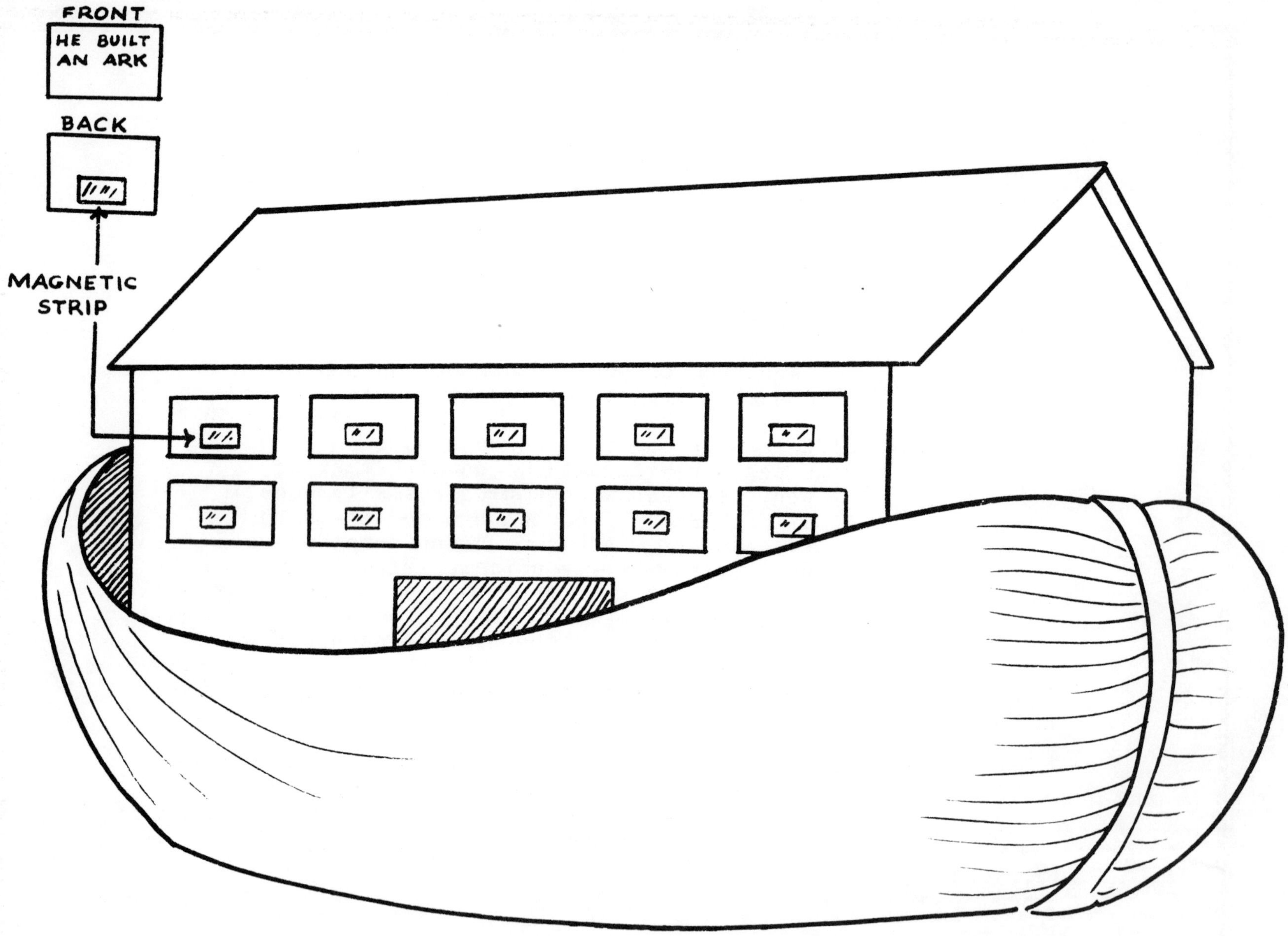
FRONT
HE BUILT AN ARK
BACK
MAGNETIC STRIP

SUBJECT: NOAH

ART ACTIVITY: Tissue collage elephant

MATERIALS: White construction paper, tissue in different colors, liquid starch, felt tip markers, hole punch, yarn, paint brushes

TEACHER PREPARATION: Prepare patterns of elephant unless children are going to cut out their own. Each child will need 2 pieces of 12" x 18" construction paper, an assortment of colored tissue paper, a bowl of starch, and a brush.

DIRECTIONS: The child will cut an elephant of two thicknesses of construction paper. Cut or tear tissue in various shapes and sizes. Brush starch over one elephant. Place tissue pieces on the elephant, overlapping until elephant is covered. Leave to dry. Repeat procedure with the other piece, making sure the elephant is facing the opposite direction. After both pieces are dry, use marker pen to fill in features. Then punch holes around the edge of the elephant, approximately 1" apart. Using the yarn, attach both pieces together by weaving the yarn in and out of the holes (may also be stapled together, if desired). A tail may be braided with yarn.

NOT ACTUAL SIZE

Noah took elephants on the ark with him. Follow these simple steps and you can draw an elephant.

STEP 1: Draw a body.

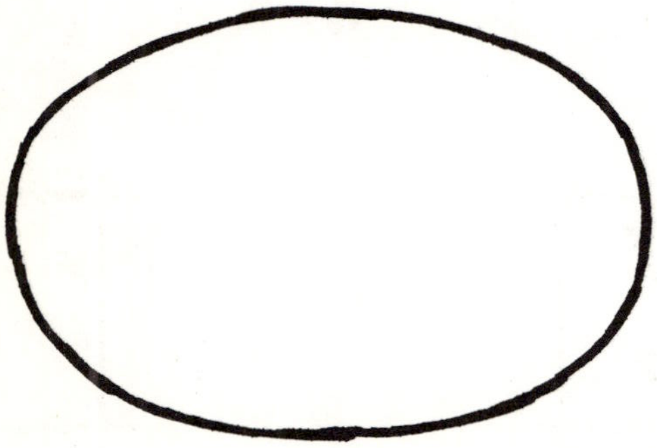

STEP 2: Add a head.

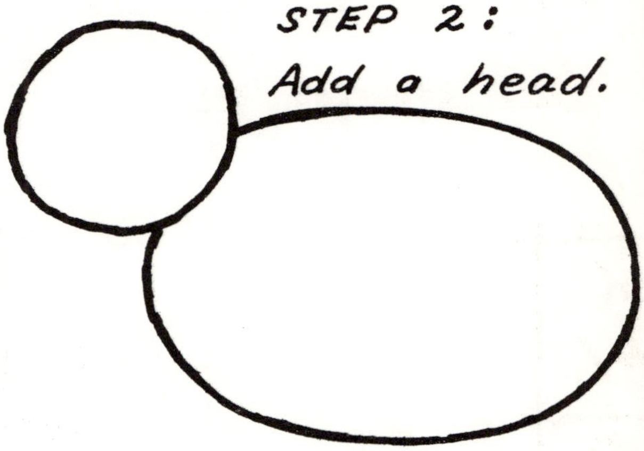

STEP 3: Add a trunk.

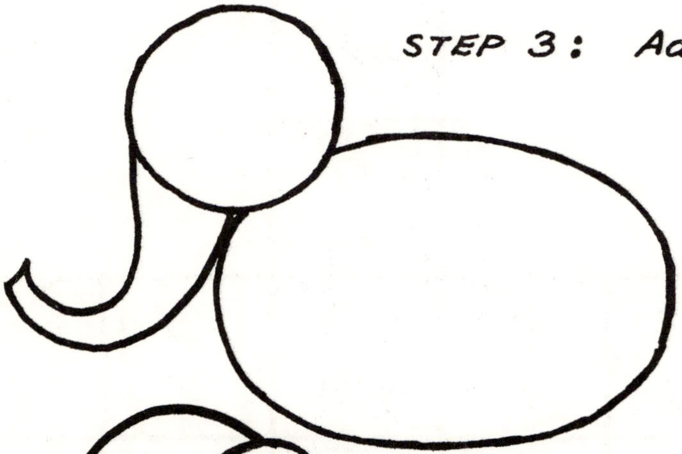

STEP 4: Add an eye, ear, legs, and a tail.

Solve these addition and subtraction problems to find out the secret message about Noah. Find the number in the diagram after you have done your math problem and then write the corresponding letter above the number on the line. Each time that number appears, the same letter is written.

4 D	0 E	2 F	6 G	1 N	10 O	12 R	11 S
5 C			7 H				13 T
8 B			16 I				15 U
3 A			9 L				14 Y

5+3 8+7 6+7 0+1 5+5 2+1 3+4 1+1 8+2 8+7 3-2 6-2

9-3 6+6 4-1 7-2 2-2 8+8 4-3 6+7 4+3 4-4 3-3 7+7 1-1 6+5

7+3 1+1 12+1 5+2 1-1 4+5 5+5 6+6 2+2

Solve this puzzle to find out what it says about Noah. Each number stands for a letter . . . 1 is A, 2 is B, etc.

16 5 15 16 12 5 23 5 18 5 12 5 1 4 9 14 7 22 5 18 25

23 9 3 11 5 4 12 9 22 5 19. 15 14 12 25 14 15 1 8

6 15 21 14 4 7 18 1 3 5 9 14 20 8 5 5 25 5 19 15 6

20 8 5 12 15 18 4. 7 15 4 20 15 12 4 14 15 1 8

1 2 15 21 20 8 9 19 16 12 1 14 20 15 4 5 19 20 18 15 25

20 8 5 23 15 18 12 4. "2 21 9 12 4 1 14 1 18 11,"

7 15 4 20 15 12 4 14 15 1 8. "25 15 21, 25 15 21 18

6 1 13 9 12 25, 1 14 4 1 16 1 9 18 15 6 5 22 5 18 25

12 9 22 9 14 7 20 8 9 14 7 23 9 12 12 7 15 9 14 20 15

20 8 5 1 18 11." 2 5 3 1 21 19 5 14 15 1 8 1 14 4 8 9 19

6 1 13 9 12 25 2 5 12 9 5 22 5 4 7 15 4, 20 8 5 25

23 5 18 5 19 1 22 5 4.

SUBJECT: ABRAHAM

BIBLE REFERENCES: Genesis 11:27-22:19

LEARNING GAME: The Bible Expert

Materials: ½ gallon milk carton, exacto knife, contact paper, poster board

Construction: Open top of milk carton completely. Cover the milk carton with contact paper. Make a 3½" slit on the front of the carton 1-3/4" from the top where the milk carton bends. Make a similar slit 1-3/4" from the bottom. Make each slit about ¼" in width. Cut poster board about 13½" x 3¼". Taper the board at one end so it fits through the bottom slit. Place the board in the milk carton, running one end through the bottom slit and under the bottom of the carton. Close the top of the carton by stapling the top of the board flush with the top of the carton. The poster board should be taut before taping it on the bottom of the carton.

Cut cards so they will fit into the slit. Write the question on the front. Write answer on back, upside down to lettering on front. Make a dot or some kind of notation in upper corner of front side of the card to indicate which edge is to be inserted first.

DIRECTIONS FOR PLAYING: The child puts card into the top slit of the "Bible Expert" with dotted side up. The card comes out the bottom slit with the answer-side up.

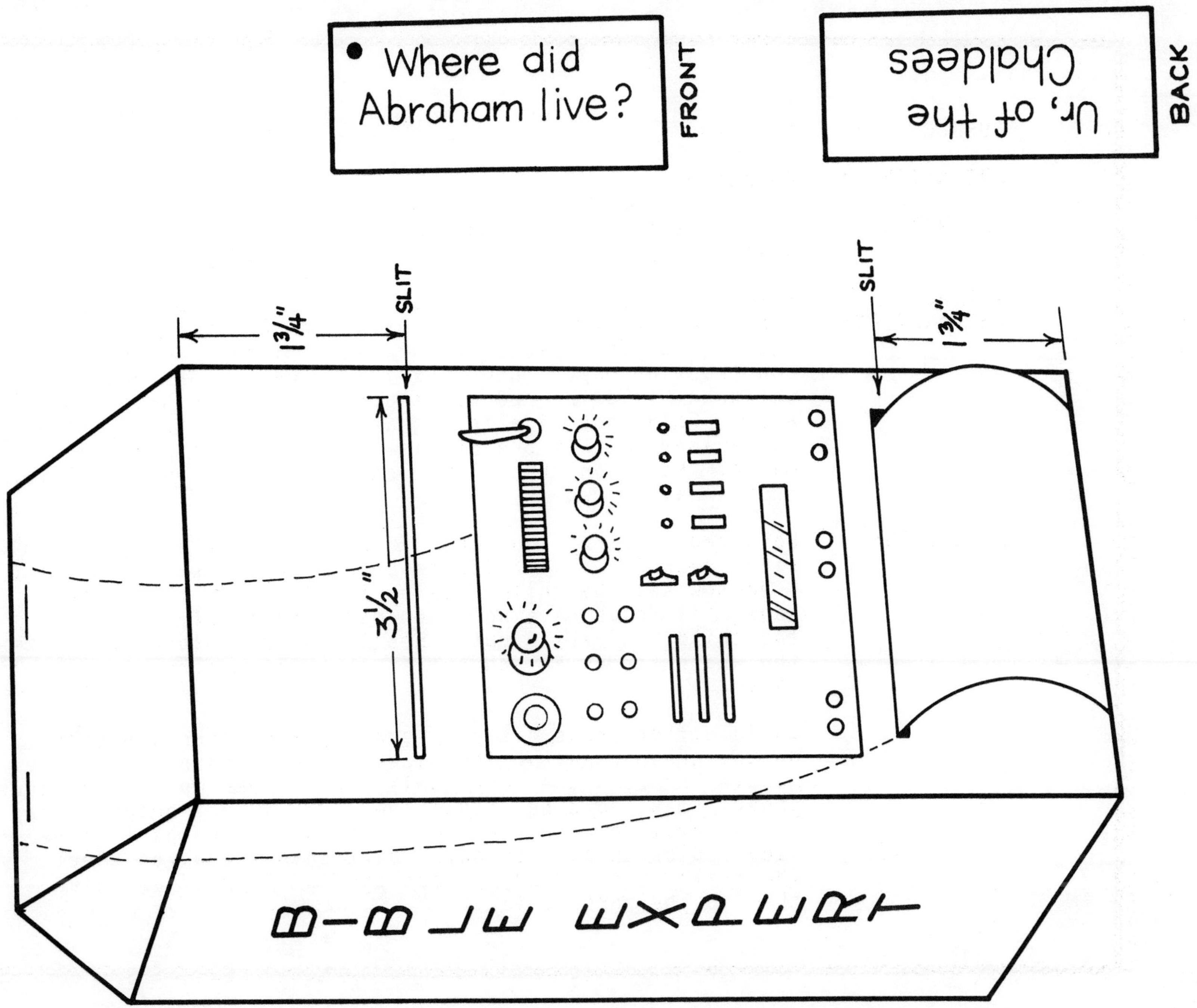
Where did Abraham live?
FRONT
Ur, of the Chaldees
BACK
SLIT
1 3/4"
SLIT
1 3/4"
3 1/2"
BIBLE EXPERT

SUBJECT: ABRAHAM

ART ACTIVITY: Cornucopia

MATERIALS: Construction paper of the following colors: green, red, white, orange, purple, yellow; scissors, glue

TEACHER PREPARATION: Make copies of a cornucopia, or child can draw his own on green construction paper. Cut white construction paper into 1½" x 12" strips, (4 for each child). Cut red construction paper into 9" x 12" pieces. For younger children, fold the red construction paper in half lengthwise. Fold each side in 1½" as a cutting guide. Unfold. Fold paper in half breadthwise, fold in half again and again. For younger children copies of patterns of different fruits may be made.

DIRECTIONS: Fold red construction paper in half lengthwise. Then fold sides over 1½". If folds have been made for the child breadthwise, the child cuts on the lines to the folded edge. If folds have not been made previously, the child is free to cut lines up to the folded edge. Weave the white strips in and out of the slits in red construction paper.

Child either draws his own cornucopia or traces pattern on the green construction paper. Then, beginning in the middle, he cuts the cornucopia-shaped hole out of the green paper. Make sure he leaves the edges intact because the green template with the shape cut out is the part to be used. Glue this green outer part onto the woven sheet. The child is now ready to cut pieces of fruit and glue them to the cornucopia.

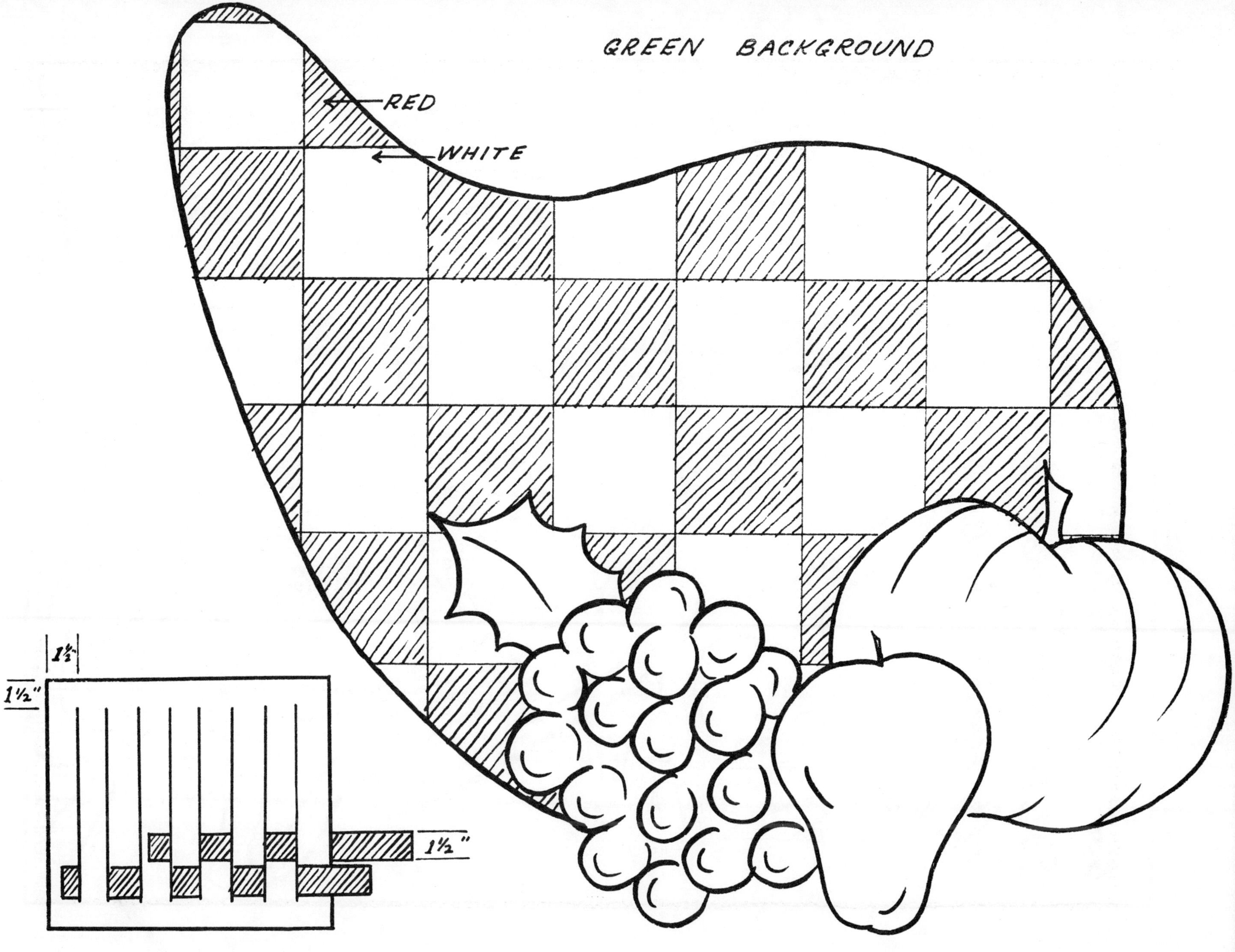
GREEN BACKGROUND
RED
WHITE
1½
1½"
1½"

God told Abraham to seek a new land. So Abraham took his family and left Haran. Help him find Canaan.

Draw lines between the pair of items that match each other . Have fun!

1.	Abraham's wife	Pillar of salt
2.	Hagar's son	Melchizedek
3.	Abraham's home	Eliezer
4.	Lot's home	Pharaoh
5.	Sacrifice of Isaac	House of God
6.	Meaning of Bethel	Sodom
7.	Egyptian king	Ur
8.	Lot's wife	Sarah
9.	Abraham's servant	Moriah
10.	King of Salem	Ishmael

(Answers in Genesis 11:27-22:19.)

Use the clues to find the A B C's of the story of Abraham (read clockwise).

A - Father of many nations

_ _ _ _ _ _ _ (Gen. 17:5)

B - The people of this place built a tower

_ _ _ _ _ (Gen. 11:9)

C - The promised land

_ _ _ _ _ _

(Gen. 17:8)

D - Ishmael and his mother were sent here when rejected by Sarah.

_ _ _ _ _ _

(Gen. 21:14)

E - Abraham lived here for a while

_ _ _ _ _

(Gen. 12:10)

F - The Lord said that if He could find _ _ _ _ _ good people in Sodom He would not destroy it. (Gen. 18:26)

G - A sinful city

_ _ _ _ _ _ _ _ (Gen. 18:20)

H - Ishmael's mother

_ _ _ _ _

(Gen. 16:15)

I - Abraham's son

_ _ _ _ _ (Gen. 21:3)

J - Lot chose the country east of this river.

_ _ _ _ _ _ (Gen. 13:11)

K - Abraham was very _ _ _ _ to his nephew.

L - Abraham's nephew _ _ _

(Gen. 11:31)

M - King of Salem

_ _ _ _ _ _ _ _ _ _ _

(Gen. 14:18)

N - Abraham's brother _ _ _ _ _

(Gen. 11:27)

O - God provided a ram for the _ _ _ _ _ _ _ _.

(Gen. 22:2)

P - Meaning of Sarah

_ _ _ _ _ _ _ _

SUBJECT: JACOB AND ESAU

BIBLE REFERENCES: Genesis 25:19-35:20

LEARNING GAME: Pick-a-pocket

Materials: Poster board, masking tape, mystic tape, felt pens, scissors

Construction: Cut 2 pieces of poster board 10" x 15". Cut 16 tagboard strips 9" x 1". Space 8 of the strips evenly on each piece of poster board. Fasten strips with masking tape across the width of the poster board, covering approximately ¼" of the bottom of each strip. After attaching each strip with masking tape, put masking tape on both sides so the strips are securely fastened and each one forms a pocket. On the left side of each strip write either "True" or "False." Use mystic tape to attach the two pieces of poster board to make a book. On 16, 4" x 2" cards write some true and some false statements about the story of Jacob and Esau. Answers may be written on the back of each card. A plastic, zippered case holding the cards can be attached to one edge of the gameboard with metal rings.

DIRECTIONS FOR PLAYING: The child determines if the statement is true or false, then puts the card in the correct pocket.

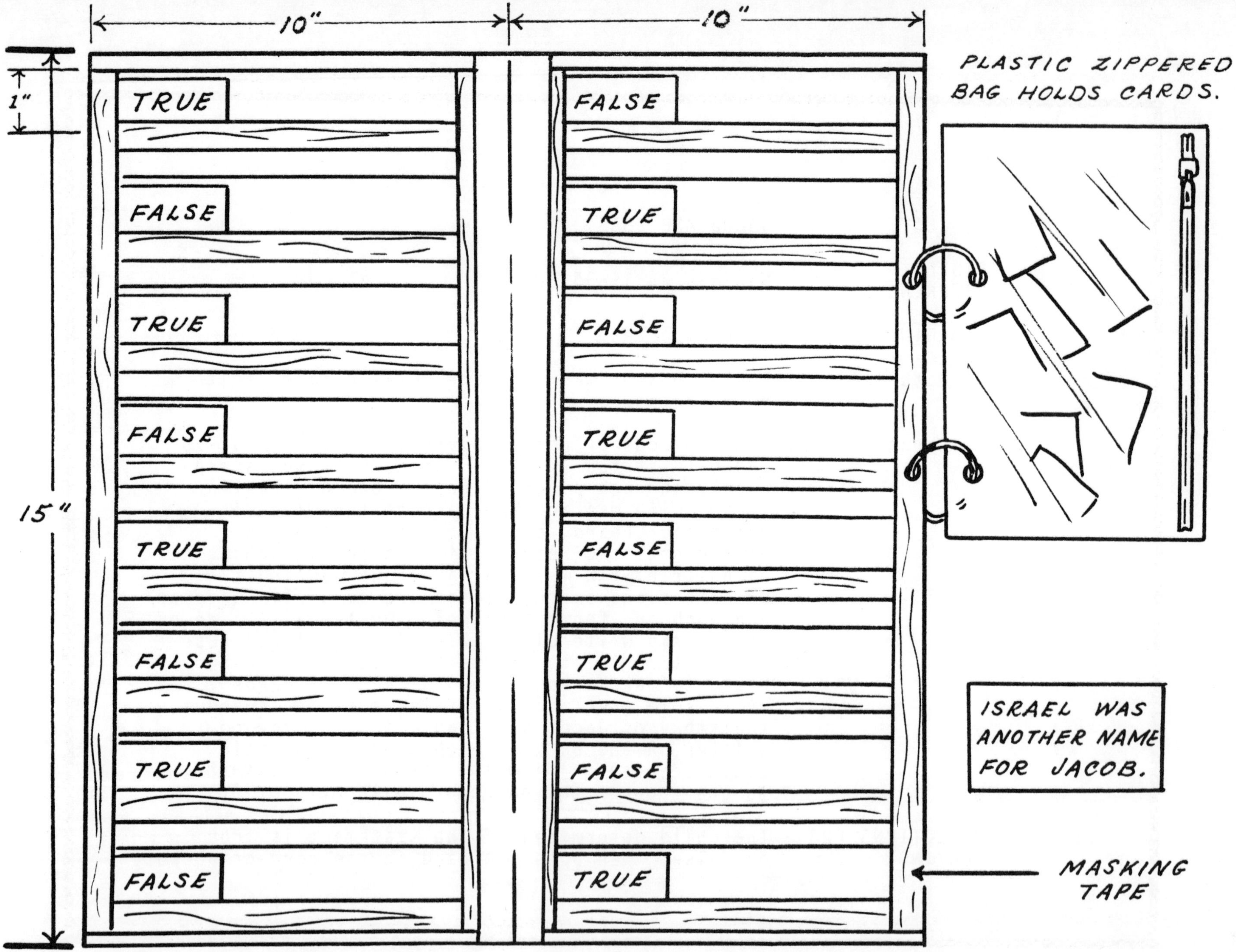
10"
10"
1"
15"
PLASTIC ZIPPERED BAG HOLDS CARDS.
TRUE
FALSE
TRUE
FALSE
TRUE
FALSE
TRUE
FALSE
FALSE
TRUE
FALSE
TRUE
FALSE
TRUE
FALSE
TRUE
ISRAEL WAS ANOTHER NAME FOR JACOB.
MASKING TAPE

SUBJECT: JACOB

ART ACTIVITY: Crayon resist

MATERIALS: Crayons, preferably primary crayons, manila drawing paper, black tempera, brushes

TEACHER PREPARATION: Dilute black tempera with water. Spread newspaper on each desk or table as child will be painting the edges of his paper.

DIRECTIONS: The child may draw his own illustration or copy the one given or the teacher may wish to make copies for very young children to color. The child will color in ladder, angels, etc. Encourage the child to use crayon heavily, making colors deep. Inform the child that whatever is not colored will eventually be black, since only the crayon will resist the paint. After the child has finished coloring the picture, he starts at the top of the page and brushes black paint across in one direction. Instruct the child not to scrub but just lightly paint over his crayoning.

Connect the dots and you will have a picture of the animals Jacob used to fool his father.
START
START

In each of the following groups, there is one word that does not belong. Circle that word. The answers can be found in Genesis 25:19-29!

1.	REBEKAH	Isaac	JACOB	Ishmael
2.	ESAU	birthright	POTIPHAR	Jacob
3.	LABAN	Haran	DANIEL	Leah
4.	RACHEL	Leah	JACOB	Esau
5.	ESAU	hunter	HAIRY	dreamer
6.	BLIND	venison	LABAN	Isaac
7.	ESAU	ladder	JACOB	angels
8.	JACOB	Abraham	BETHEL	dream
9.	ESAU	supplanter	JACOB	Rachel
10.	RACHEL	Benjamin	JACOB	Esau

1. Gen. 25:25 2. Gen. 25:20 3. Gen. 25:26 4. Gen. 24:29 5. Gen. 31:13

Jacob and Esau

Unscramble the letters in the names below.

1. A E S U

2. K E B R E H A

3. B A J C O

4. B A N A L

5. L E T B H E

6. L E R H A C

7. H E A L

8. J N I E A B M N

9. L I S R E A

10. A C A I S

6. Gen. 29:16 7. Gen. 29:23 8. Gen. 35:18 9. Gen. 32:28 10. Gen. 26:12

SUBJECT:	JOSEPH
BIBLE REFERENCES:	Genesis 37:1-50:26
LEARNING GAME:	Pyramid Power
Materials:	Tagboard, felt pens, scissors
Construction:	Draw a pyramid. Make slits on opposite sides (see illustration). Write parts of a story on strips that will fit in the slits. On the back of each strip, write a numeral corresponding to the order in the story.
DIRECTIONS FOR PLAYING:	The child will take the strips and endeavor to put the story in the correct sequence.

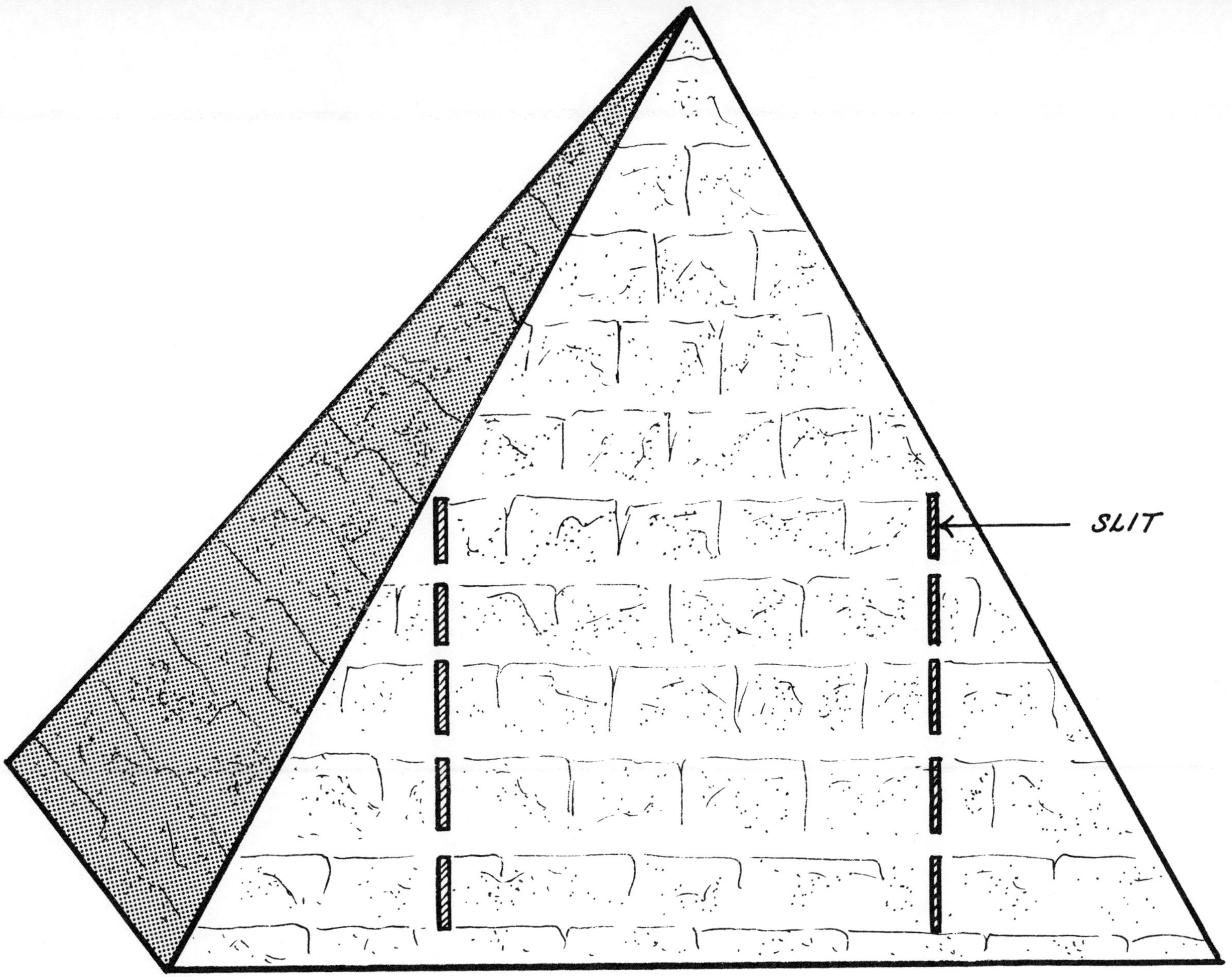

JOSEPH'S BROTHERS
THREW HIM INTO A PIT.

IN THIS STRANGE LAND
JOSEPH WAS A SLAVE.

SUBJECT:	JOSEPH
ART ACTIVITY:	Blotto print
MATERIALS:	2 or 3 colors of tempera paint, paint brushes, 9" x 12" white construction paper, scissors
TEACHER PREPARATION:	Prepare paint in bowls, one for two children. For younger children, fold white 9" x 12" in half.
DIRECTIONS:	Fold white construction paper in half. Unfold. With paintbrush child will place 2-3 drops of paint of each color on the fold. Then fold paper as at the beginning. With fist press on fold and rub toward the edges so paint will spread. Allow to dry for a few minutes. Trace coat pattern or draw freehand on blotto print. Cut coat shape.

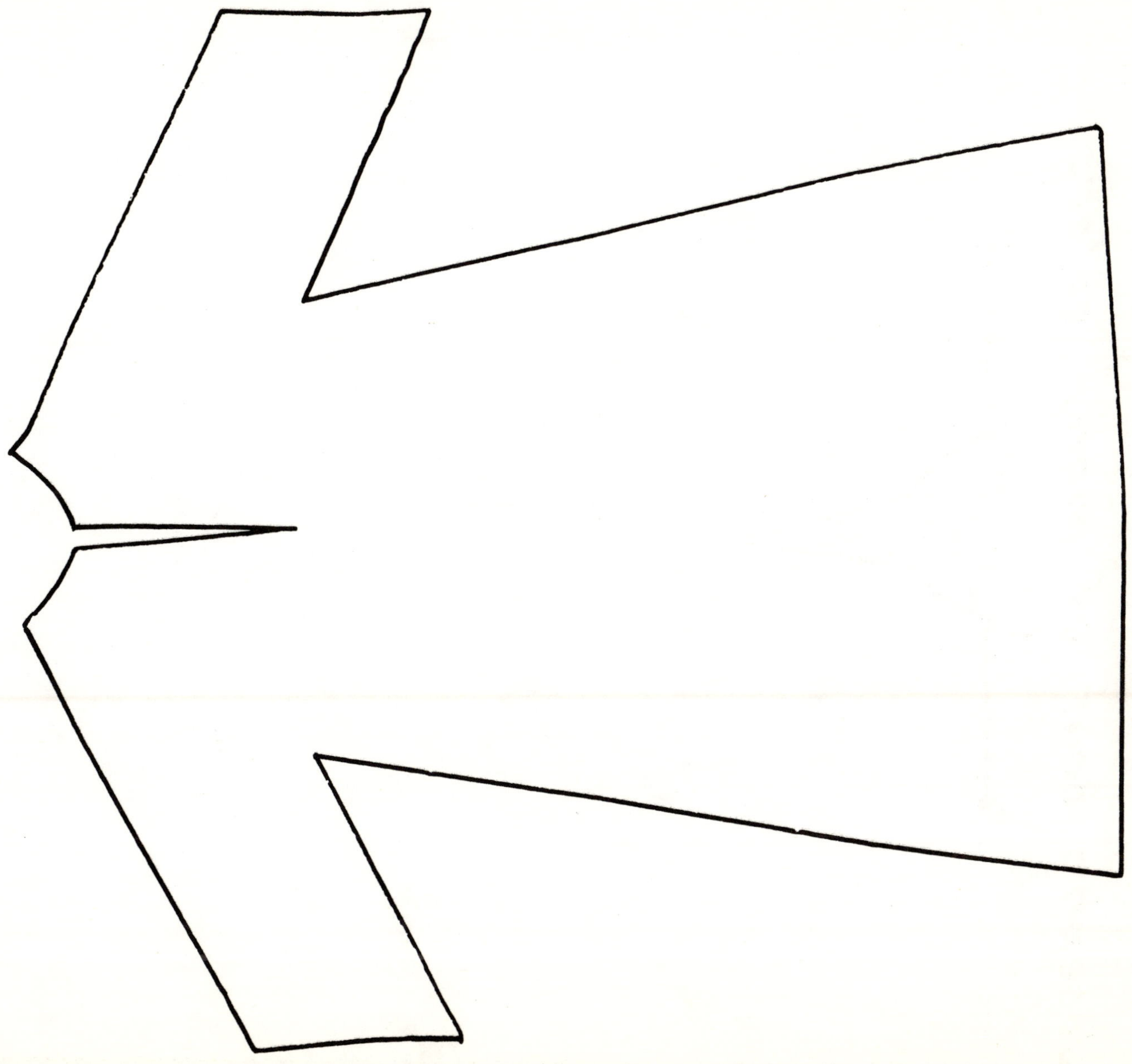

Connect the dots to finish drawing Joseph's coat of many colors.

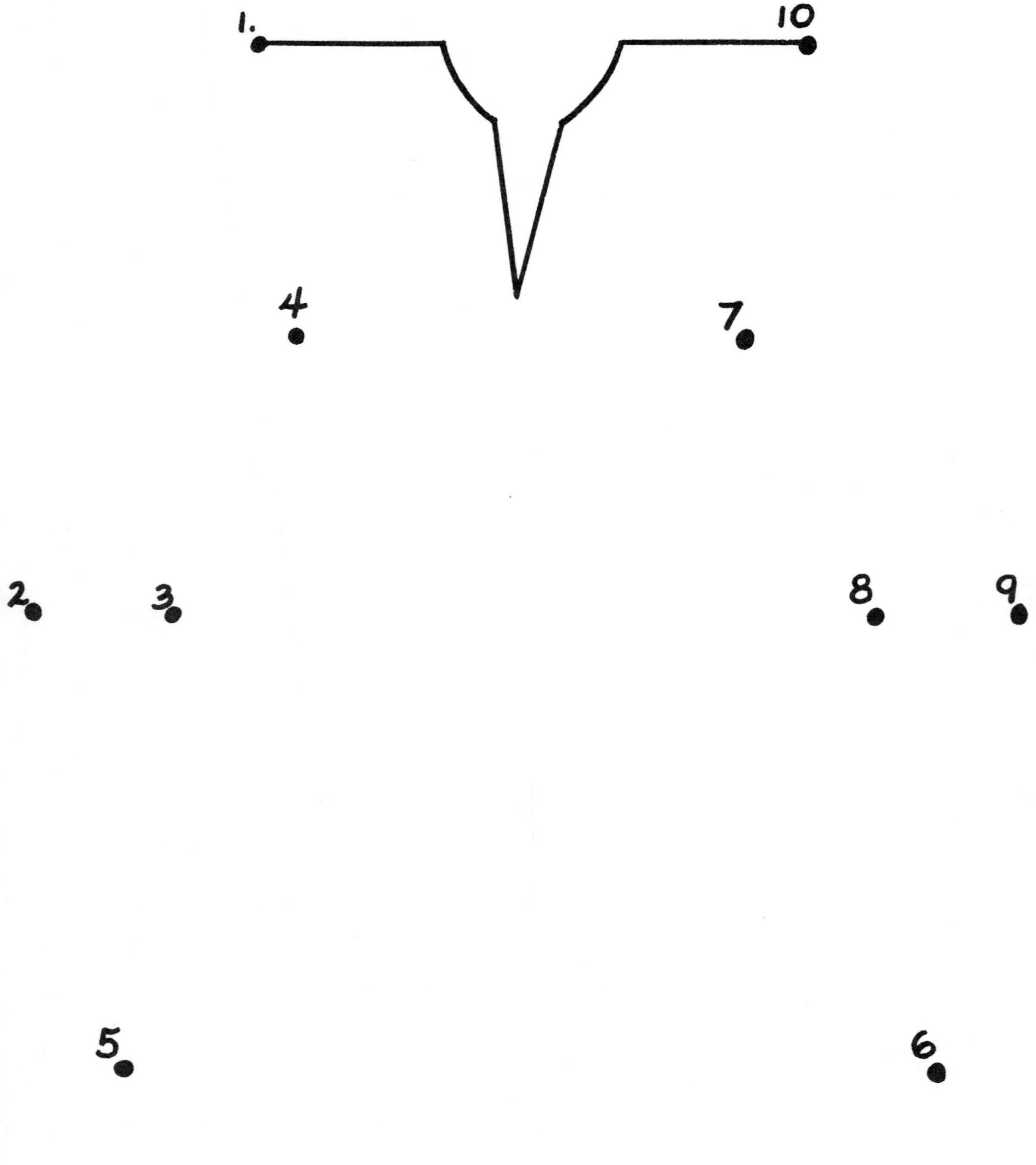

Here are some sentences that tell part of the story of Joseph. Arrange them in the correct order by numbering from 1 to 10. (Genesis 37:3, 13-36).

____ One day Jacob sent Joseph in search of his brothers.

____ Joseph put on his colorful coat and began the journey.

____ They were going to Egypt to sell slaves.

____ Jacob had given Joseph a coat of many colors.

____ When the brothers saw Joseph afar off they thought of a plot to get rid of him.

____ After a while, some Arabs on camels passed by.

____ They threw him into a pit after stripping him of his coat of many colors.

____ That gave the brothers an idea.

____ The brothers then took Joseph's coat and dipped it in the blood of an animal so that it would look as though a wild animal had attacked Joseph.

____ They lifted Joseph out of the pit and handed the Arabs twenty pieces of silver.

Rewrite the following story, correcting the errors. (Genesis 37:3-27)

Jacob loved Benjamin the most out of his 10 sons. Because Jacob loved Benjamin the most, the brothers were jealous. They were jealous of Joseph, too.

One night Reuben had a nightmare. He told his brothers about it. It was about sheaves bowing down to his sheaf.

Joseph also had a dream. In his dream he saw the sun, moon, and five stars bowing down before him.

Jacob and his family lived at Hebron. Jacob's flocks were so large that there was not enough pasture nearby. One day Jacob sent his 10 sons to Shechem with the flocks. After some time Jacob sent Joseph in search of them.

When the brothers saw him, they rejoiced. They helped take off his coat and ate lunch together.

SUBJECT:	MOSES
BIBLE REFERENCES:	Exodus (Exodus 1:1--Deuteronomy 34:12)
LEARNING GAME:	Crossing the Red Sea
Materials:	Poster board, felt pens, scissors, tagboard, magnetic strips, construction paper
Construction:	Draw or use construction paper to make scene of Red Sea with path in center of the Sea, making it broad enough for 2 rows (or more, if desired) of magnetic strips (see illustration). Cut construction paper figures to represent people. Attach magnetic strips to the back of each figure. Cut 30, 2" x 3" cards from tagboard. Write questions pertaining to the lesson on the cards. On a separate sheet list answers.
DIRECTIONS FOR PLAYING:	Cards are shuffled and placed face down. Each child playing chooses a figure. One child turns a card over and answers the question. If he is right, he may move his figure across one stepping-stone. The one to cross the Red Sea first wins.

MAGNETIC STRIPS

SUBJECT: MOSES

ART ACTIVITY: Decoupage

MATERIALS: Sandpaper, wood pieces about 8" x 10" and ½" thick, copies of the Ten Commandments, paint brushes, decoupage finish

TEACHER PREPARATION: Spread newspaper on tables. Pour decoupage finish (available in most craft stores) into containers so children can have easy access to it. Smooth the wood pieces with sandpaper. Make copies of the Ten Commandments (see illustration).

DIRECTIONS: With paint brush spread decoupage finish evenly over wood. Lay copy of Ten Commandments on the wood, centering it and smoothing it to make sure there are no air bubbles. Apply another coat of finish or as many as desired. Three usually are sufficient. A coat of shellac may be applied when print is completely dry.

The Ten Commandments

I

Thou shalt have no other gods before me.

II

Thou shalt not make unto thee any graven image.

III

Thou shalt not take the name of the Lord thy God in vain.

IV

Remember the sabbath day, to keep it holy.

V

Honour thy father and thy mother.

VI

Thou shalt not kill.

VII

Thou shalt not commit adultery.

VIII

Thou shalt not steal.

IX

Thou shalt not bear false witness.

X

Thou shalt not covet.

Exodus 20:3-17

Moses sent 12 spies into the Land of Canaan. Can you find them in this picture?

How well can you climb up and down these word ladders? Read each clue and fill in the missing letters.

1. Mountain on which Moses received the Ten Commandments. (Ex. 19:20) __ __ N A __
2. Holy of Holies (Ex. 25:9) __ __ __ __ __ N A __ __ __
3. Food in the wilderness (Ex. 16:15) __ __ __ N A
4. Promised Land (Ex. 16:35) __ __ N A __ __
5. Aaron's son (Ex. 28:1) N A __ __ __

1. God's chosen people (Ex. 3:10) __ __ R A __ __
2. Moses' wife (Ex. 2:21) __ __ __ __ __ R A __
3. Ruler of Egypt (Ex. 6:11) __ __ __ R A __ __
4. Animal offered for sacrifice (Ex. 29:15) R A __
5. A city in Egypt where the Israelites worked (Ex. 1:11) R A __ __ __ __ __

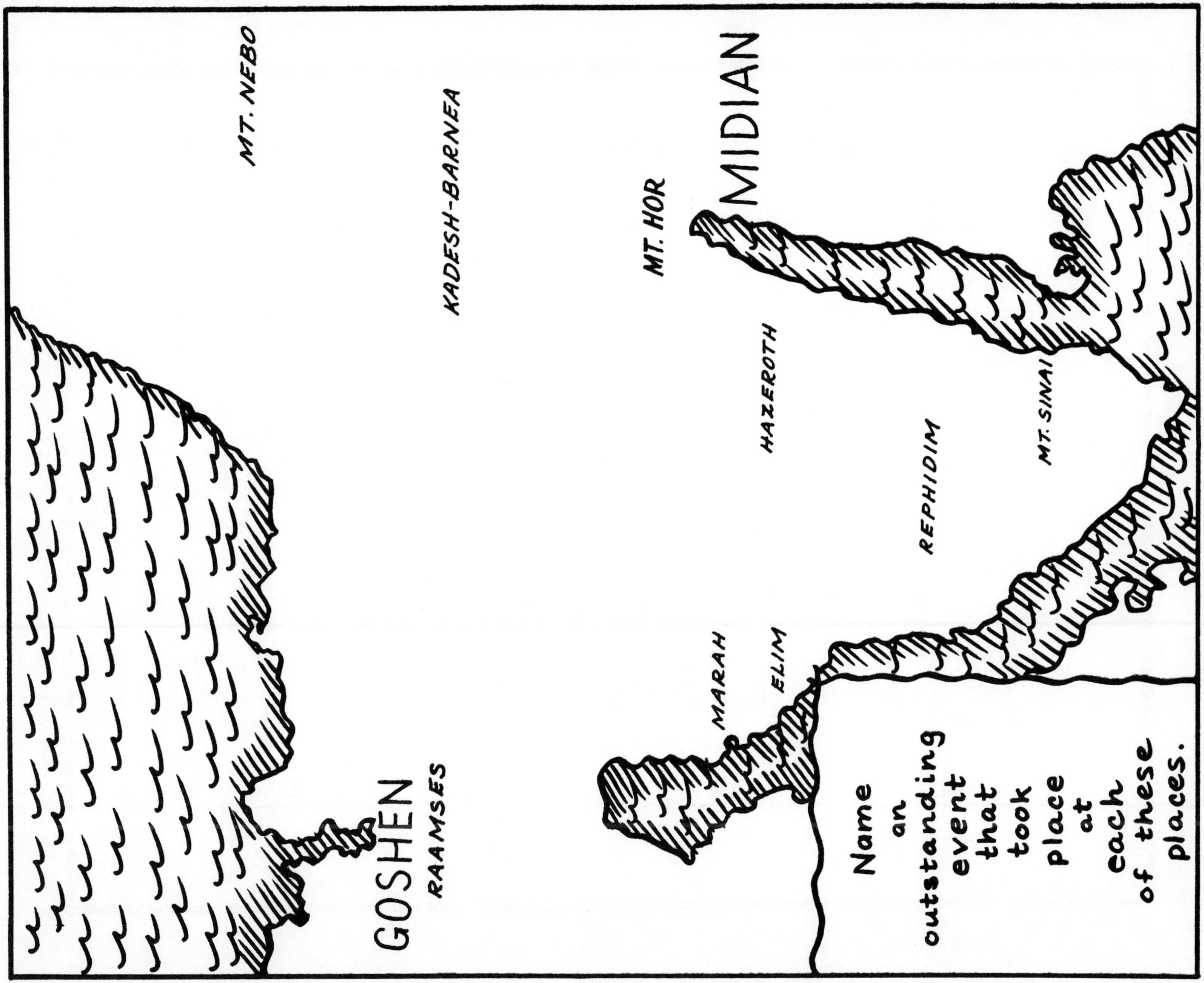
MT. NEBO
KADESH-BARNEA
MT. HOR
MIDIAN
HAZEROTH
REPHIDIM
MT. SINAI
MARAH
ELIM
GOSHEN
RAAMSES
Name an outstanding event that took place at each of these places.

SUBJECT:	JOSHUA
BIBLE REFERENCES:	Joshua 1:1-24:30
LEARNING GAME:	The Bright Touch
Materials:	Plywood or masonite (size will vary depending on how many items you intend to use on the board), drill, copper or brass nuts and bolts (must be copper or brass for good conduction), battery case and batteries*, electrical leads*, 2 volt wire*, indicator light*, receptacle for light*, cup hooks, tagboard, hole punch.
Construction:	Sketch layout of board on plywood or masonite with pencil. Make cards to be matched. Punch holes in tops so these can be hung on cup hooks. This allows you to change the items to be matched. On the board, drill holes and screw in hooks for cards. Below each card, drill hole and screw in bolt. Attach leads and batteries to back of board. Mount receptacle for light bulb at top of board. Attach wires to nuts of matching items. See illustration.
DIRECTIONS FOR PLAYING:	The child touches one lead to bolt under each matching item. If correct, light goes on.

*These are available at electronics stores such as Radio Shack.

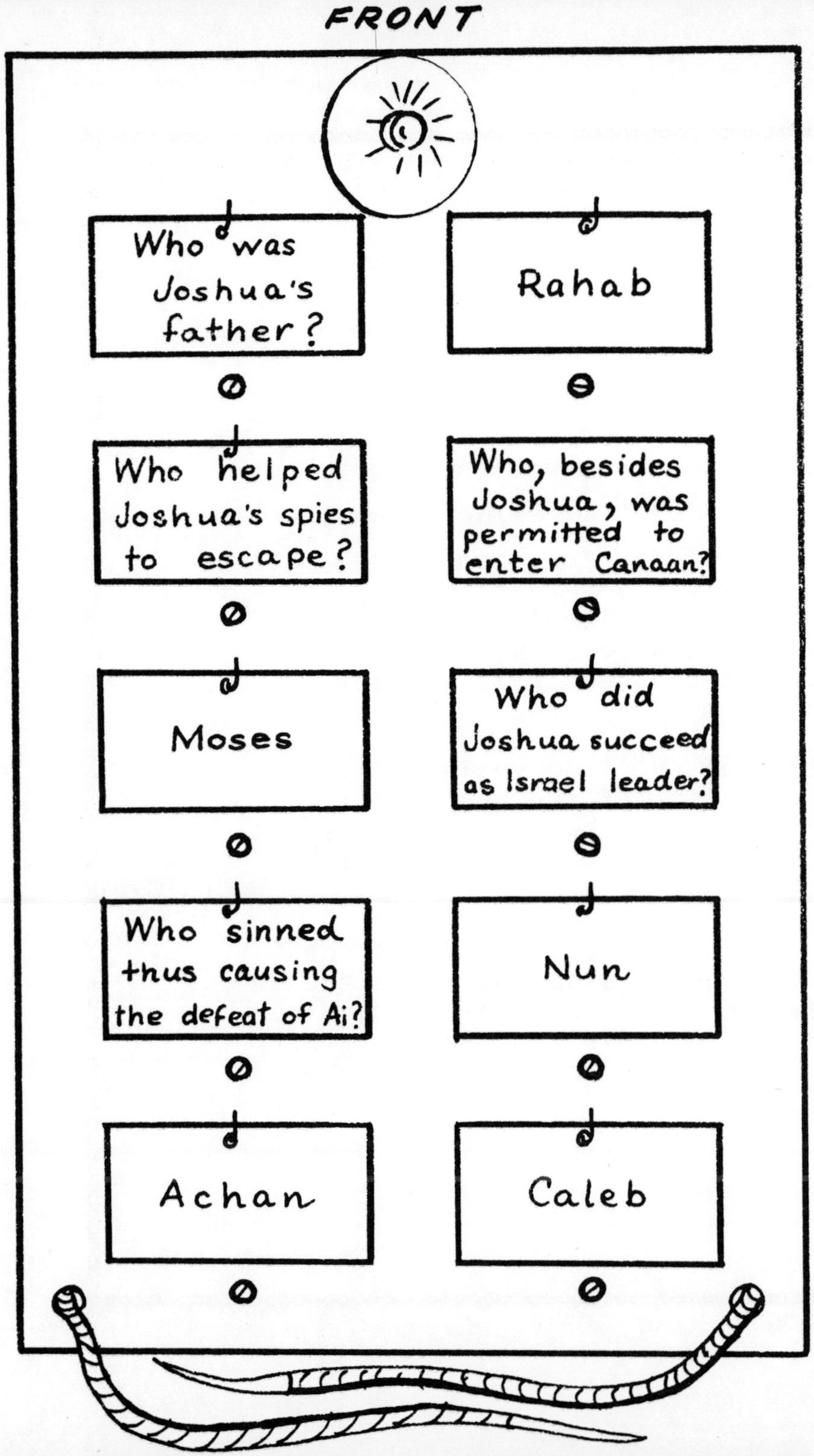
FRONT
Who was Joshua's father?
Rahab
Who helped Joshua's spies to escape?
Who, besides Joshua, was permitted to enter Canaan?
Moses
Who did Joshua succeed as Israel leader?
Who sinned thus causing the defeat of Ai?
Nun
Achan
Caleb

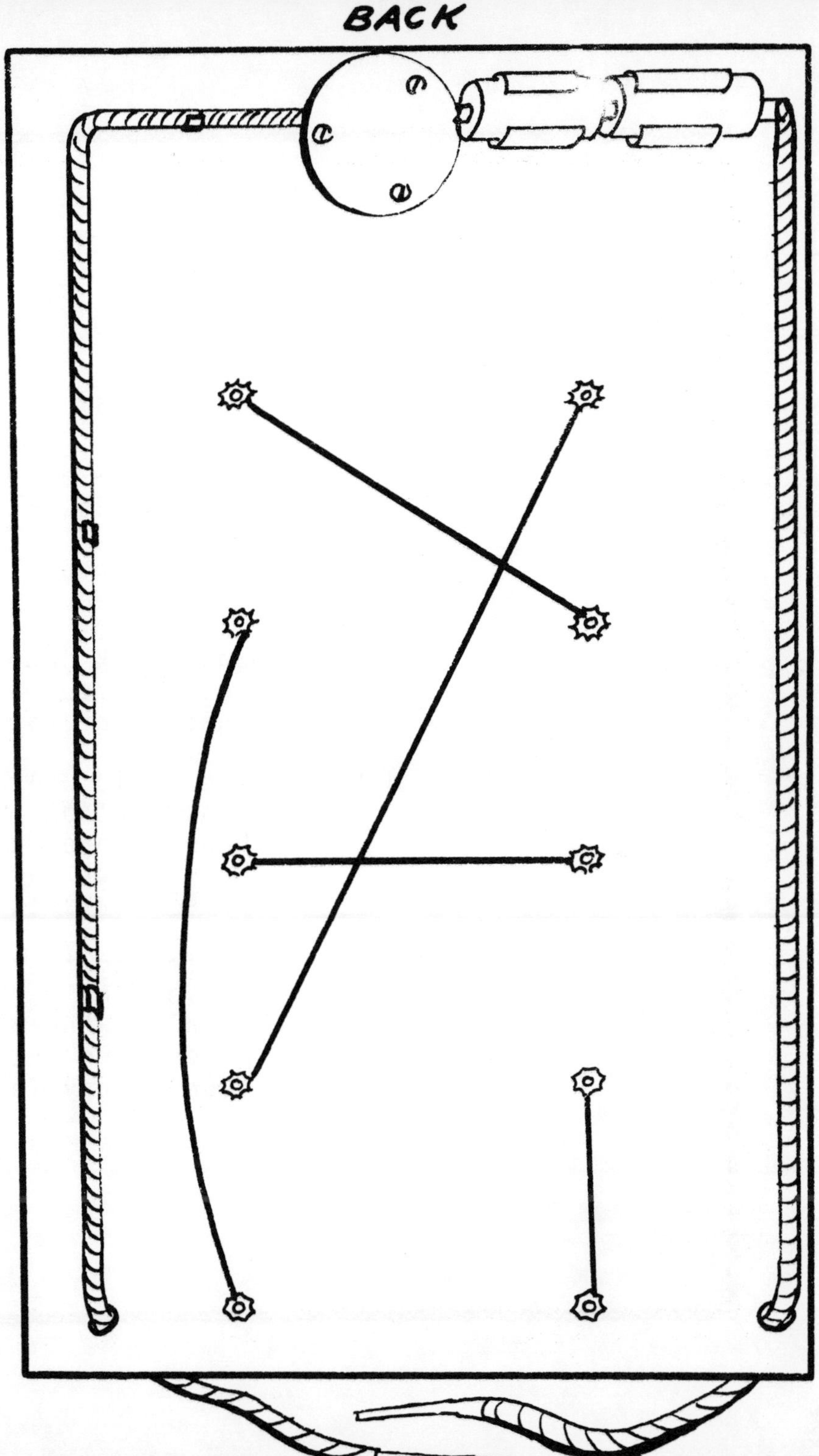
BACK

SUBJECT: JOSHUA

ART ACTIVITY: Sun mobile

MATERIALS: Yellow, orange, and black construction paper, yarn, scissors, glue, tagboard

TEACHER PREPARATION: Make tagboard patterns of sun for each child, if desired. (Older child may make his own pattern). Cut yarn into 18" lengths. Cut orange and black paper into 3" squares, two for each child. You will also need 2, 9" x 12" yellow sheets for each child.

DIRECTIONS: The child will trace and cut from yellow construction paper two sets of the sun rays. From orange paper pieces, cut two small circles. From black paper pieces, cut two sets of "happy face" features.

Paste together the two orange circles, with one end of the yarn sandwiched inside. Leaving enough yarn for the orange circle to hang in the middle, place yarn between two sun rays and glue together. Glue "happy face" features on the orange circles.

The walls of Jericho came tumbling down. Copy the letters on the rocks in the boxes below in the right order and you will find out who led the people around the city.

☐	☐	☐	☐	☐	☐
1.	2.	3.	4.	5.	6.

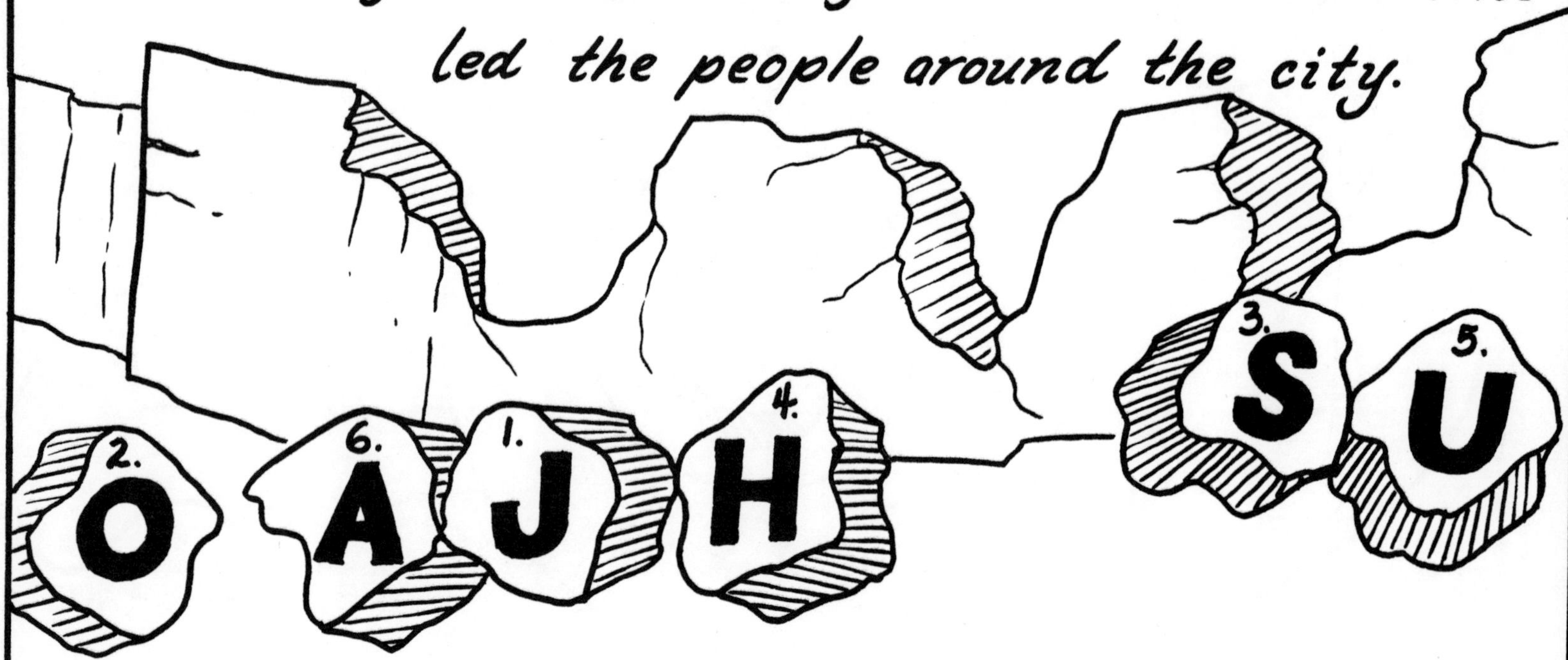

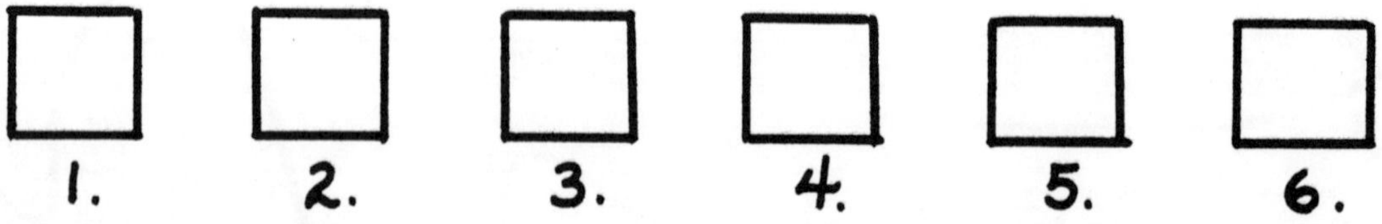

Unscramble the letters in the names below, one letter to each square. Then arrange the shaded letters to form the missing word.

Joshua followed the Lord's ______________.

TESIROMA

SHENAAMS

COHIREJ

DAJRNO

SHJAOU

SEMSO

IEARSL

BACLE

NANACA

NACAH

Fill in the missing vowels to complete these names.

M __ S __ S (Joshua 1:1)

J __ S H __ __ (Joshua 1:1)

R __ H __ B (Joshua 6:17)

C __ L __ B (Joshua 15:13)

J __ R __ C H __ (Joshua 6:1)

J __ R D __ N (Joshua 3:14)

__ S R __ __ L __ T __ S (Joshua 3:17)

C __ N __ __ N (Joshua 14:1)

__ C H __ N (Joshua 7:1)

G __ B __ __ N (Joshua 10:2)

S H __ L __ H (Joshua 18:1)

SUBJECT:	SAMSON
BIBLE REFERENCES:	Judges 13:1-16:31
LEARNING GAME:	Answer Holes
Materials:	Tagboard, felt pens
Construction:	Draw shape of lion (or any other simple shape) on tagboard (see illustration). Punch holes about 1½" from the edge, approximately 2" apart. On one side write questions, each question adjacent to a hole. On the other side, write the answers corresponding to the questions on the front.
DIRECTIONS FOR PLAYING:	Two can play. One child takes a pencil and pokes it through any hole. He reads the questions and gives the answer to the question near that hole. The student on the other side checks the answer.

Whom were the Philistines worshiping?
What was the secret of Samson's strength?
What was Samson's father's name?
Who deceived Samson into telling his secret?
What did the Philistines do to Samson?
What was the answer to Samson's riddle?

SUBJECT:	SAMSON
ART ACTIVITY:	Cut-and-paste lion
MATERIALS:	Construction paper of the following colors: brown, yellow, black, white, red; scissors, glue
TEACHER PREPARATION:	Each child will need the following: 1, 9" x 9" brown construction paper 1, 6" x 6" yellow construction paper 2, 2" x 3" yellow construction paper 1, 7" x 3" white construction paper 1, 2" x 3" black construction paper 1, 1-1/2" x 1-1/2" red construction paper
DIRECTIONS:	Round off corners of brown construction paper. Fringe all around. Round off corners of 6" yellow square for face. Paste in center of brown construction paper. Cut ears, eyes, nose, mouth, and tongue, and paste down. (See illustration.)

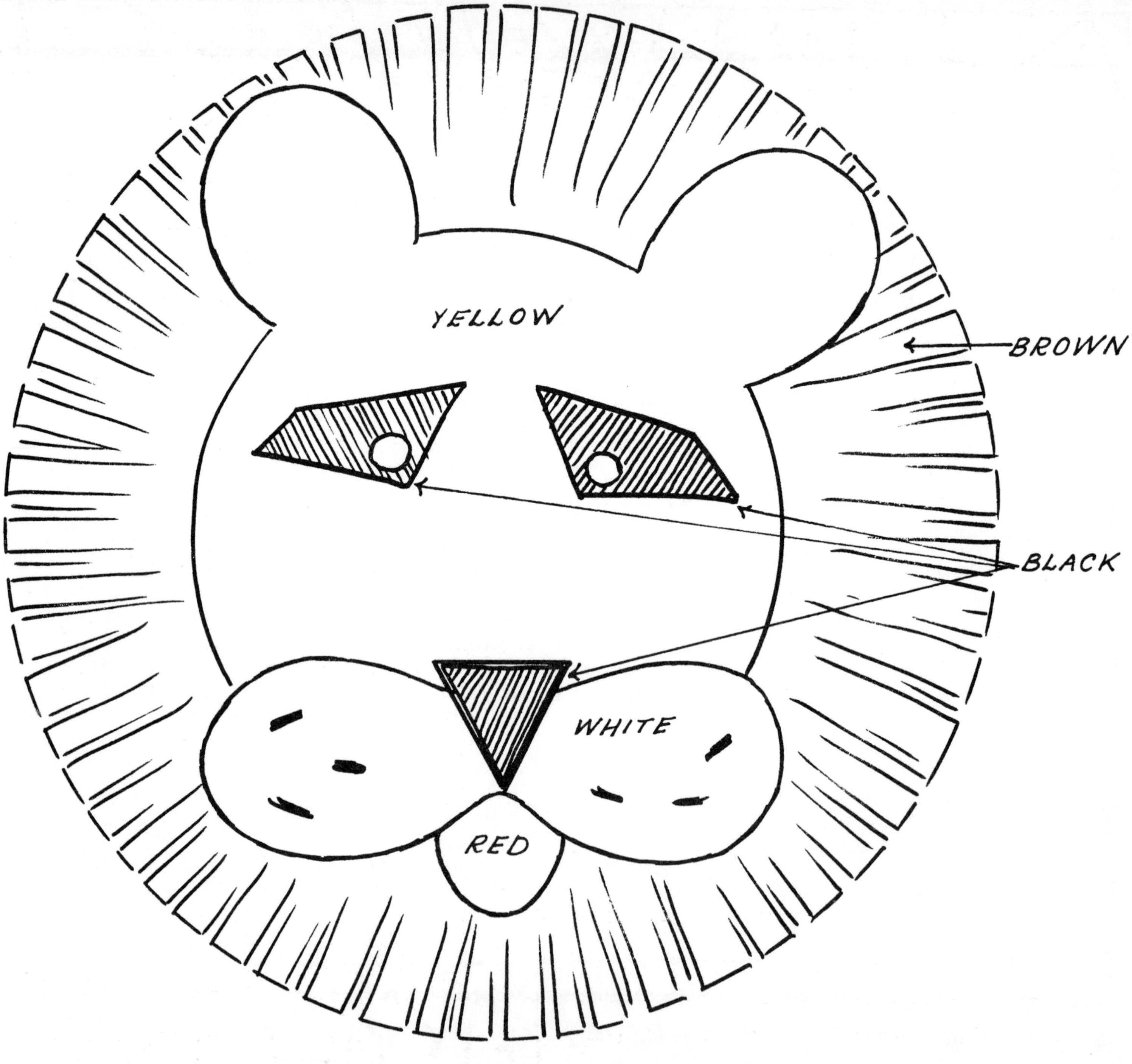
YELLOW
BROWN
BLACK
WHITE
RED

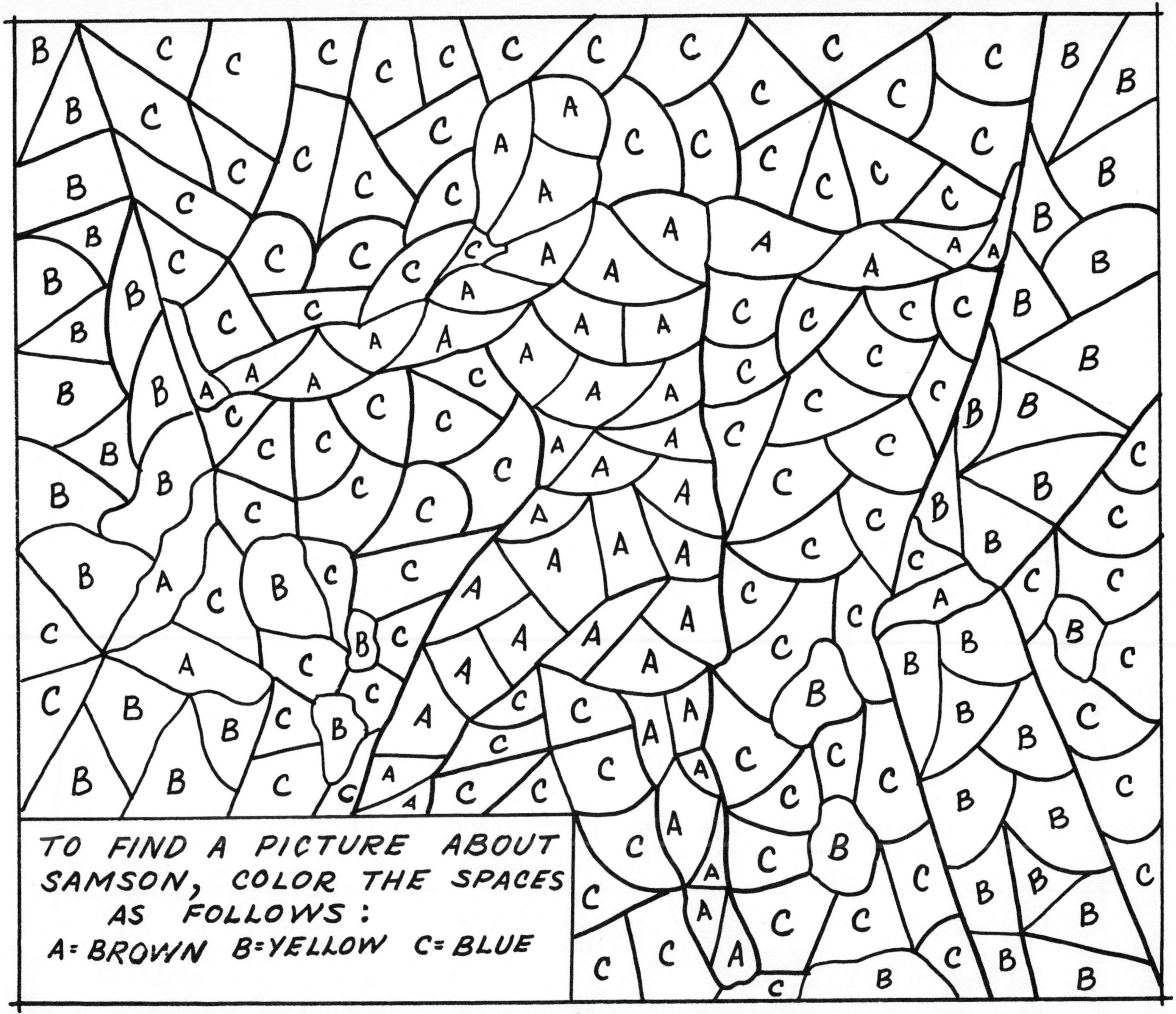

TO FIND A PICTURE ABOUT SAMSON, COLOR THE SPACES AS FOLLOWS:

A=BROWN B=YELLOW C=BLUE

Choose a word from the list below and fill in the blank for the appropriate sentence. A few extra words are in the list to make it a bit more challenging for you! Read Judges 13-16 for clues.

Manoah	Nazarite	Jericho
Noah	Mennonite	tiger
Delilah	Timnah	lion
Dagon	hair	honey
Samuel	Moses	arms
judge	Deborah	Philistines
priest	Amorites	molasses

1. Samson was born a ______________________.
2. Samson's father was ____________________.
3. Samson was a ___________________ for many years.
4. Samson's strength lay in his __________________.
5. The _____________________ were anxious to find out the secret of his strength.
6. ___________________ was a girl Samson loved.
7. The heathen god that was being worshipped at the time was ______________.
8. Samson's first girlfriend was from the city of __________________.
9. Samson killed a _______________ with his bare hands.
10. When he passed the animal again after a few days he found _____________ in its body, which satisfied his hunger.

Break the code and learn a fact about Samson.

FIRST: Fill in the blanks below.

SECOND: Write the first letter of the word you fill in on the line with the number under it next to the sentence.

THIRD: Find that number in the code below and write the corresponding letter above it. Each time that number appears in the code the same letter is written.

1. This activity sheet is about ____________________. ___ 36

2. The father of Samson was ____________________. ___ 14

3. An angel appeared to Manoah's ____________________. ___ 25

4. Judges 14:1 tells us Samson went to ____________________. ___ 12

5. There he saw a woman who was a daughter of the __________. ___ 10

6. Judges 14:19 tells us Samson went to ____________. ___ 8

7. Samson called the place where he threw the jawbone ______. (Judges 15:17) ___ 6

8. Three thousand men of Judah went to the rock __________. (Judges 15:11) ___ 21

9. Delilah cut Samson's ____________________. ___ 2

10. Judges 16:1 tells us Samson went to ______________________. ___ 9

11. Samson never cut his hair because he was a ______________. ___ 15
(Judges 16:17)

12. Samson judged ______________________ for 20 years. ___ 5

13. Manoah gave a meat ____________________ to the Lord when the angel visited. (Judges 13:19) ___ 4

36 8 14 36 4 15 36   36 12 6 4 15 9   10 4 5 15 12   25 8 36

2 5 36   36 12 6 21 15 9 12 2.

SUBJECT: SAMUEL

BIBLE REFERENCES: 1 Samuel 1:1-25:1

LEARNING GAME: Stand up and Match

Materials: Triple thickness cardboard or plywood, tagboard, felt pens, glue

Construction: Cut cardboard or plywood into the following pieces: 1, 15" x 4"; 1, 15" x 3"; 1, 15" x 2". Cover these with contact paper. Glue the 15" x 2" piece upright flush with one end of the I5" x 4" piece. Glue the 15" x 3" piece about ¼" in front of the 15" x 2" thus making a stand. Glue ½" x 2" strips at 3-1/8" intervals on top of the 15" x 4" base (see illustration). Cut 3" x 4" cards. On each of them write a question on top and the answer on the bottom. Then make 3" x 2" cards to correspond with the 3" x 4" cards. Write the answers that have been written already on the 3" x 4".

DIRECTIONS FOR PLAYING: The child places his cards in the stand and matches the smaller cards to them. Then he lifts up his card to see if it is right. Only when the card is lifted can the answer be seen.

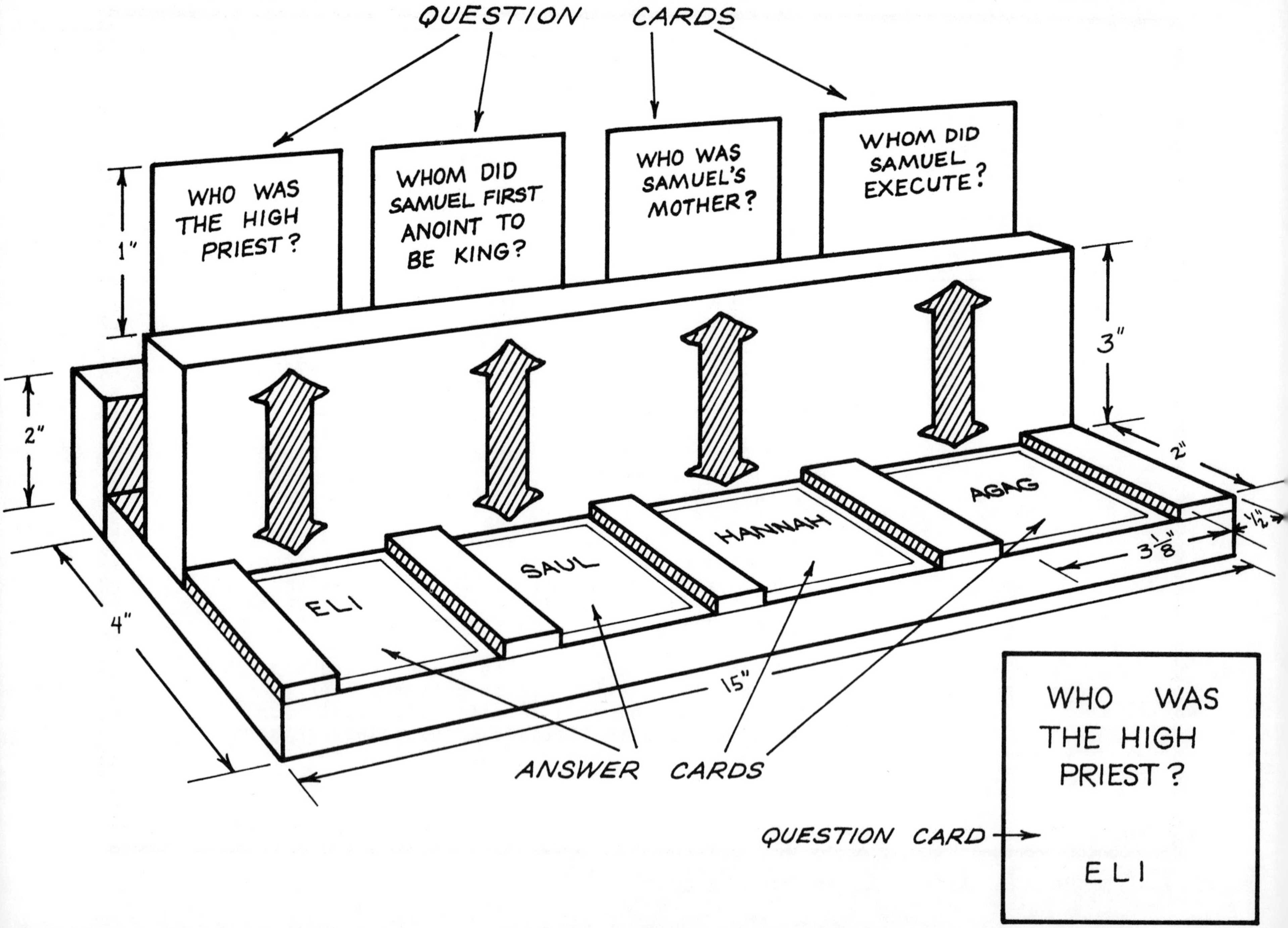
QUESTION CARDS
WHO WAS THE HIGH PRIEST?
WHOM DID SAMUEL FIRST ANOINT TO BE KING?
WHO WAS SAMUEL'S MOTHER?
WHOM DID SAMUEL EXECUTE?
1"
3"
2"
2"
1/2"
3 1/8"
4"
15"
ELI
SAUL
HANNAH
AGAG
ANSWER CARDS
WHO WAS THE HIGH PRIEST?
QUESTION CARD
ELI

SUBJECT:	SAMUEL
ART ACTIVITY:	Silhouette of child in prayer
MATERIALS:	White and black construction paper, scissors, glue
TEACHER PREPARATION:	For primary children, make copies of the illustration.
DIRECTIONS:	Trace outline of child in prayer on the black construction paper. Cut and glue on white. Intermediate children can cut silhouettes of their friends.

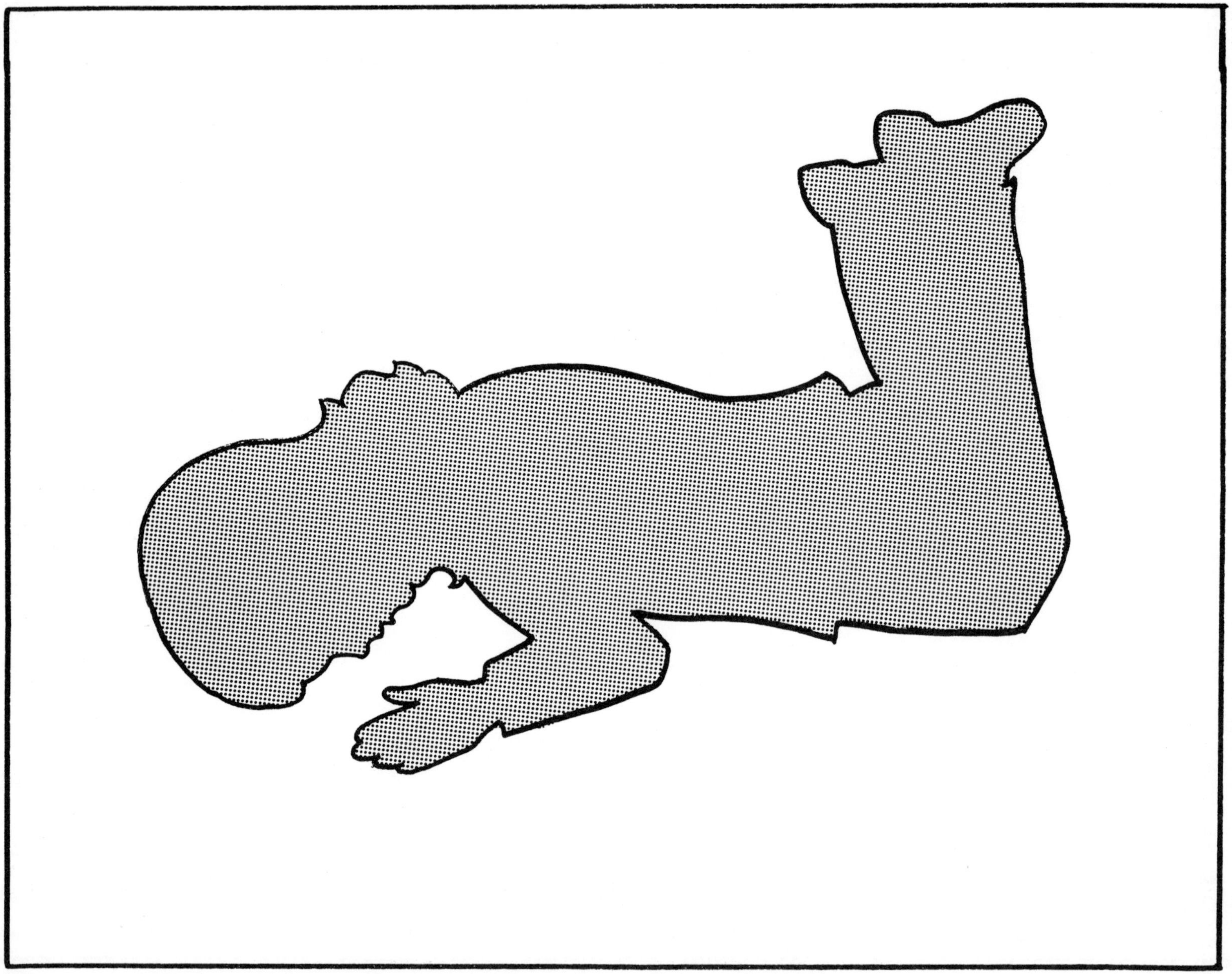

Here are some things that happened in the story of Samuel. Cut the pictures out and paste them below in the correct order.

1st 2nd 3rd 4th

WHO AM I?

1. I am a priest.
   I took care of a little boy.
   He later became a prophet.
   Who am I? (1 Sam. 1:9)

2. I am a little boy.
   I was called by God to serve Him.
   When I became a prophet, I anointed Saul.
   I also anointed David.
   Who am I? (1 Sam. 3:20)

3. I wanted a child very much.
   I asked God to give me one.
   I promised God to dedicate my child to Him.
   Who am I? (1 Sam. 1:9-11)

4. I belong to the Philistines.
   They worship me.
   Who am I? (1 Sam. 5:3-4)

5. I am a Levite.
   The Ark was placed in my house.
   Who am I? (1 Sam. 7:1)

6. I am a man.
   I had a son who was dedicated to God before he was born.
   Who am I? (1 Sam. 1:23)

The story of Samuel is written below in his name. Rewrite it in paragraph form.

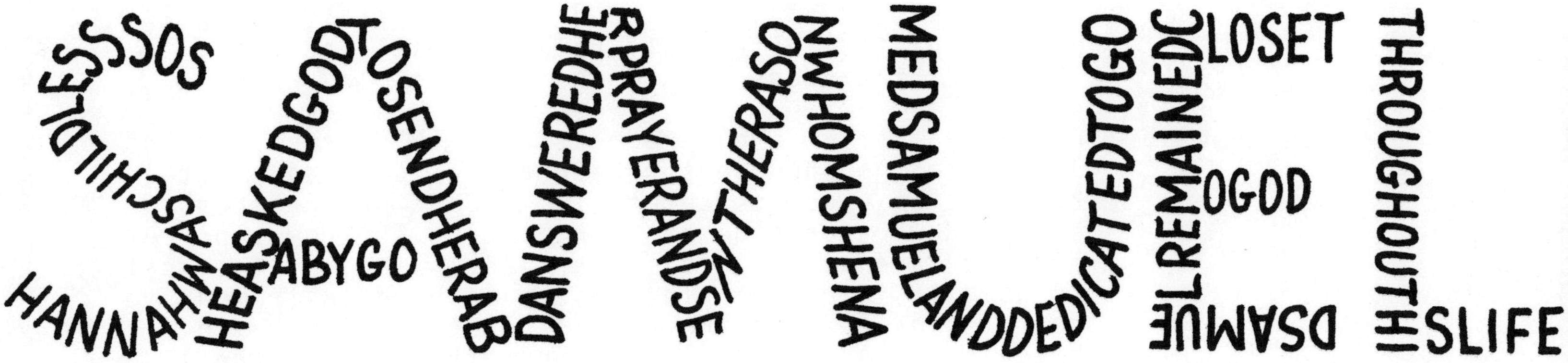
HANNAHWASCHILDLESSSOS
HEASKEDGODTOSENDHERAB
ABYGO
DANSWEREDHE
RPRAYERANDSE
NTHERASO
NWHOMSHENA
MEDSAMUELANDDEDICATEDTOGO
DSAMUE
LREMAINEDC
LOSET
OGOD
THROUGHOUTHI
SLIFE

SUBJECT: DAVID

BIBLE REFERENCES: 1 Samuel 16:1-1 Kings 5:11

LEARNING GAME: Lace-ups

Materials: Stiff cardboard, 1" wide masking tape, solid color contact paper, plastic-tipped shoelaces (8), compass or any pointed instrument, ruler, plastic acetate, tagboard, felt pens

Construction: Cut a vest from cardboard measuring 10" across and 16" down from the shoulders. Decorate as desired. Cut 2 strips of plastic acetate 13" x 3¼". Place these strips down each side of board, about 1" from top. Use masking tape along both sides (lengthwise) of the acetate to hold it in place. Then use a pointed instrument to punch holes next to the acetate on each side. The first hole is approximately 1-3/4" from the top and the 7 succeeding holes are approximately 1¼" apart. After holes are punched, push shoelace through each hole on just one side and then tie a knot in the shoelace on the underside. Now cut tagboard strip 14" x 2". Write items to be matched on one strip making sure the spacing of the items matches the holes on the vest. On the other strip write the corresponding items in a different order, again making sure the items are spaced so they match the holes.

DIRECTIONS FOR PLAYING: The child slides strips under the acetate and then uses the shoelaces to show the matching items.

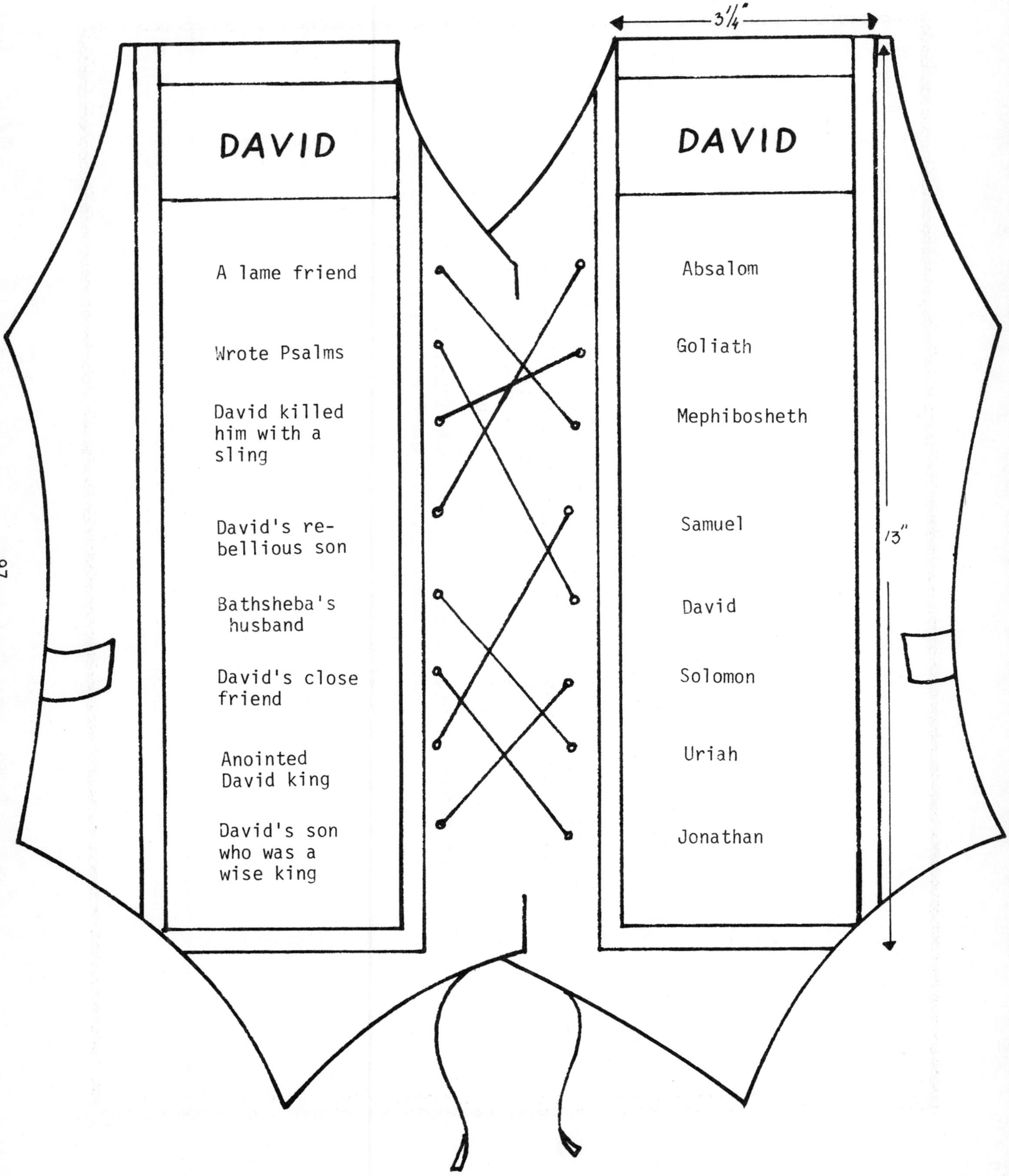
3¼"
13"
DAVID
A lame friend
Wrote Psalms
David killed him with a sling
David's re-bellious son
Bathsheba's husband
David's close friend
Anointed David king
David's son who was a wise king
DAVID
Absalom
Goliath
Mephibosheth
Samuel
David
Solomon
Uriah
Jonathan

SUBJECT:	DAVID
ART ACTIVITY:	Pretzel writing
MATERIALS:	Pretzel sticks, regular (round) pretzels, glue, construction paper (12" x 18")
TEACHER PREPARATION:	Place 5 or 6 pretzels of each kind on table so that each child will have his own supply. Prepare sample for children. Glue pretzels on construction paper, making "The Lord is my Shepherd," biting off extraneous bits of pretzels.
DIRECTIONS:	Show sample to children. Children will usually know what to do from there. Be sure to have them place the letters before gluing.

THE LORD IS MY SHEPHERD

SUBJECT: DAVID

ART ACTIVITY: Felt banner

MATERIALS: Felt of 2 contrasting colors, glue, dowel stick, yarn, scissors, needles

TEACHER PREPARATION: Make letter patterns for "The Lord is my Shepherd," or child can cut his own (see directions for cutting letters without a pattern). For each child provide the following:

1, 16" x 20" piece of felt
1, 10" x 14" piece of contrasting color felt
1, 19" dowel stick
1, 50" length of yarn
1 needle

DIRECTIONS: Fold the narrow end of the 16" x 20" piece of felt over approximately 1". Iron. This will make it easier for the class to sew the top. Cut letters for the verse. Place the letters on felt piece; trace and cut. Glue the letters in place on banner. With yarn, sew the top of the banner with a running stitch. Put dowel stick through. Tie yarn around one end of the dowel stick. Leaving enough yarn to hang the banner, tie yarn to the other end of the dowel stick.

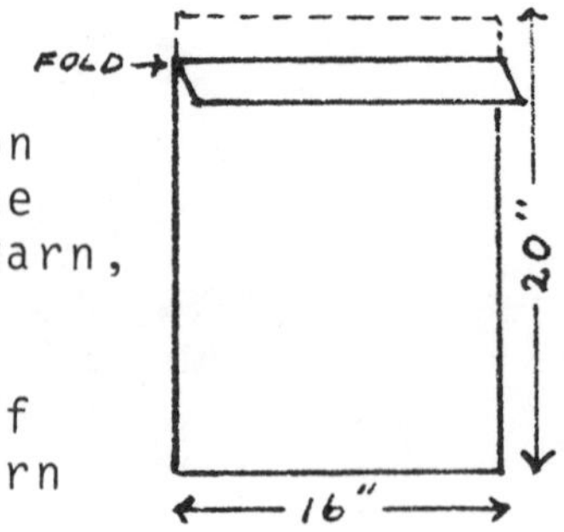

BLOCK CUT LETTERS

FOLD ON DOTTED LINES ----

CUT ON SOLID LINES ——

Use O pattern for O, Q, C, G

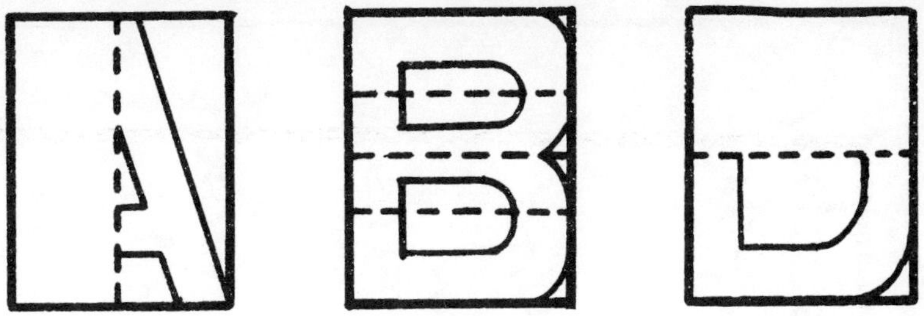

A B D

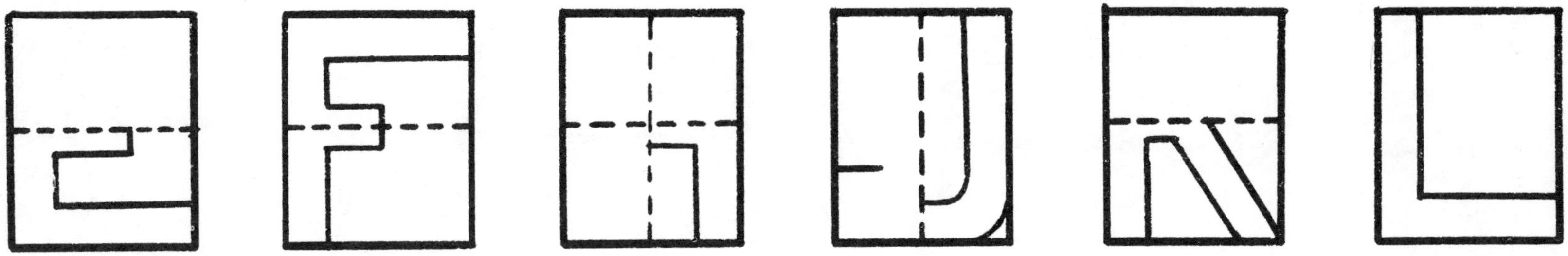

E F H J K L

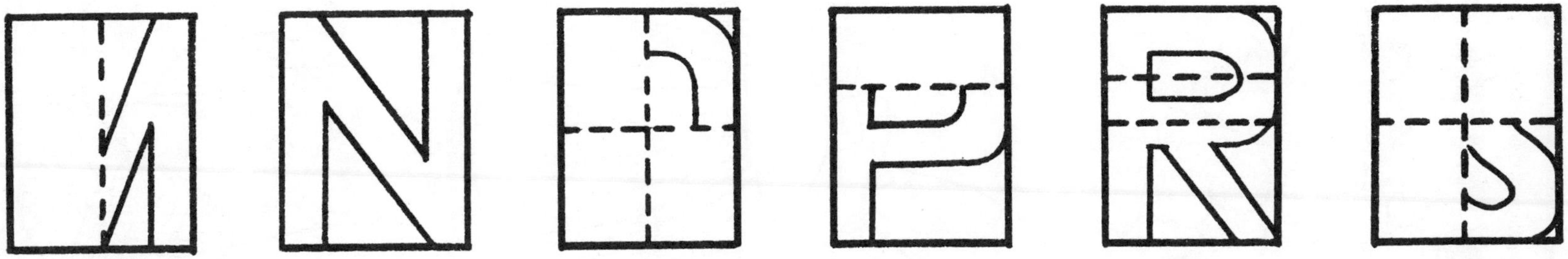

M N O P R S

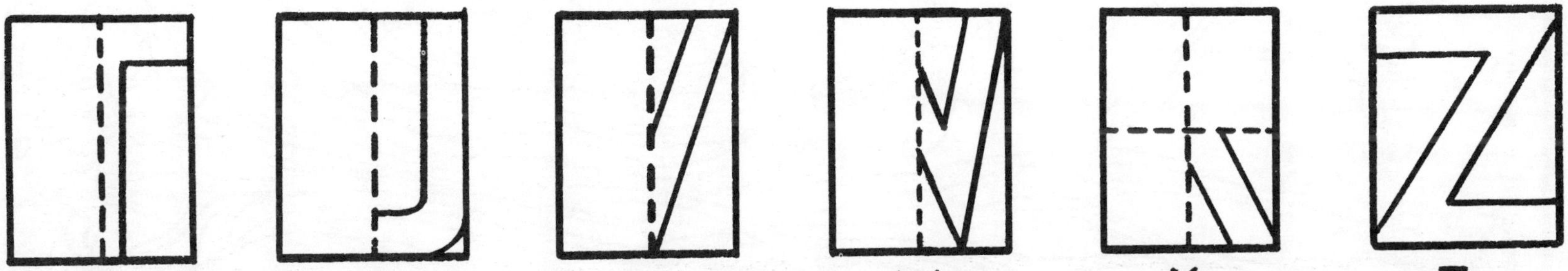

T U V W X Z

In this picture, 6 items that were important in the life of David are hidden.
Can you find:
1. DAVID'S BOW
2. SAUL'S JAVELIN
3. DAVID'S HARP
4. DAVID'S SLING
5. GOLIATH'S SWORD
6. DAVID'S CROWN

Unscramble the words (some of the words appear more than once). Then cross out all the letters <u>except</u> the middle letter of each word. Now find the secret message and write it on the line below.

1. dad
   tah
   eev
   eip
   dad

6. ypupp
   sytud
   tac
   lil
   yommm
   kas

2. eaw
   ear
   eot
   eat
   evt

5. eat
   ehs
   tes

3. ratme
   taf
   yufnn
   yee

4. oet
   fof

_ _ _ _ _   _ _ _ _ _   _ _ _ _   _ _   _ _ _   _ _ _ _ _ _ .

1.   2.   3.   4.   5.   6.

David had a good friend named Mephibosheth. See if you can find names of other people and things in the story of David that begin with each letter of the name, "Mephibosheth." Have fun reading the clues!

M __ __ __ __ __ (1 Sam. 18:20)

E __ __ __ __ __ __ (1 Sam. 7:1)

P __ __ __ __ __ __ __ __ __ __ (1 Sam.17:3)

H __ __ __ __ __ (2 Sam. 5:3)

I __ __ __ __ __ __ __ __ __ (1 Sam.13:20)

B __ __ __ __ __ (1 Sam. 7:4)

O __ __ (1 Sam. 10:1)

S __ __ __ (1 Sam. 9:17)

H __ __ __ __ __ (2 Sam. 15:37)

E __ __ __ __ __ __ __ (1 Sam. 7:12)

T __ __ __ __ __ __ __ __ __ (2 Sam.6:17)

H __ __ __

M = Saul's daughter; E = Took care of the Ark; P = Enemies of the Israelites; H = Where David was made king; I = God's chosen people; B = Heathen god; O = Used for anointing; S = King before David; H = David's advisor; E = "Here the Lord helped us" T = Place of worship H = Another word for hear

SUBJECT:	ELIJAH
BIBLE REFERENCES:	1 Kings 17:1-2 Kings 2:11
LEARNING GAME:	Clip the Cruse
Materials:	Cardboard, felt markers, clothespins
Construction:	Make "cruse of oil" from cardboard. Divide into as many parts as desired. Write questions on one side and corresponding answers on the back. Write answers on clothespins.
DIRECTIONS FOR PLAYING:	The child clips the clothespin to the cardboard, with answer facing down. After the child has clipped all of them the answers can be checked. The answer on the clothespin should be in the same place as the answer on the back of the cardboard.

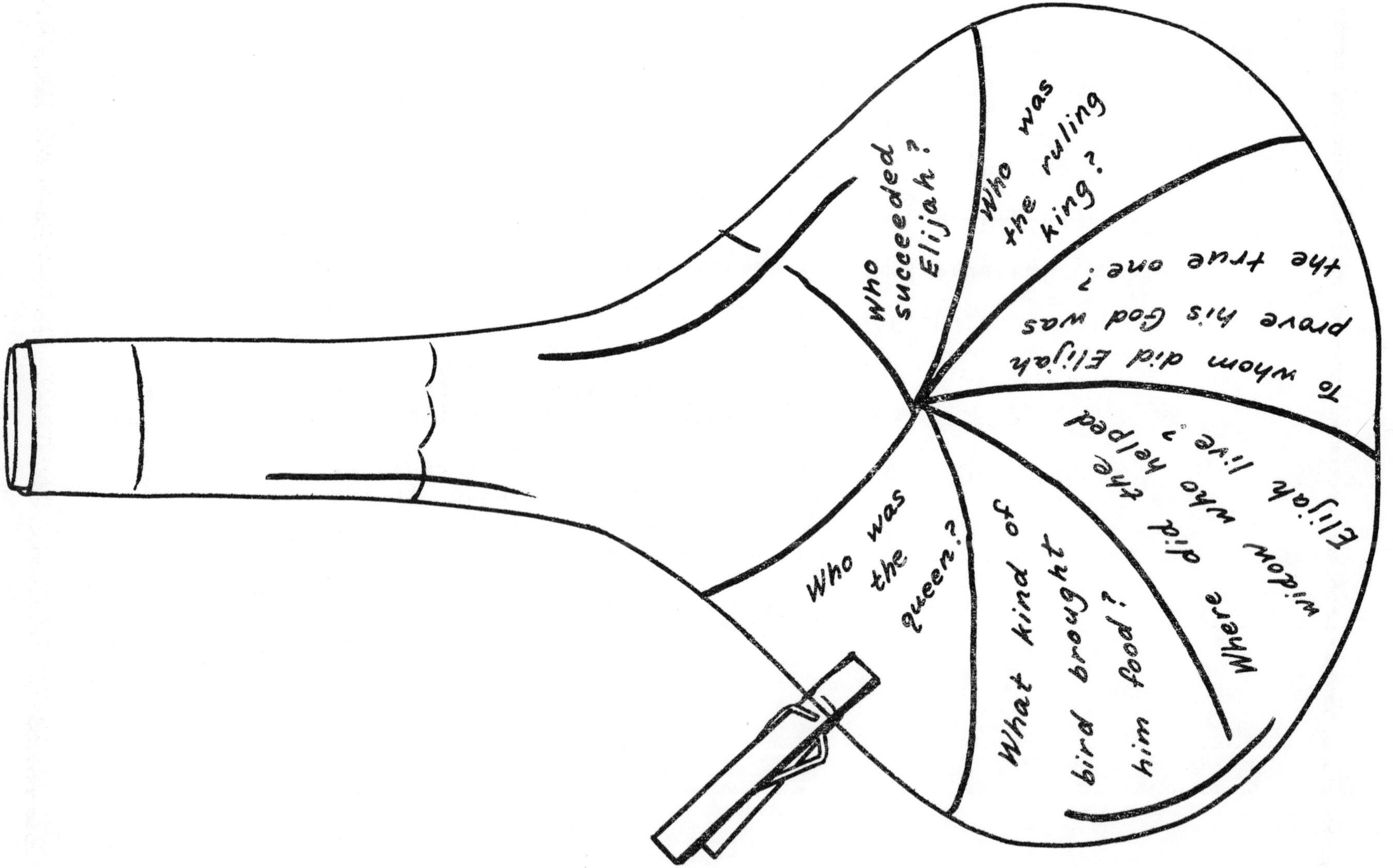
Who succeeded Elijah?
Who was the ruling king?
To whom did Elijah prove his God was the true one?
Where did the widow who helped Elijah live?
What kind of bird brought him food?
Who was the queen?

SUBJECT:	ELIJAH
ART ACTIVITY:	Raven
MATERIALS:	Black construction paper, black tissue (optional), scissors, glue
TEACHER PREPARATION:	Make copies of bird pattern (see illustration).
DIRECTIONS:	Trace bird pattern on black paper. Cut. Make a slit in the bird where indicated. Slip wings through slit. Cut feathers from tissue. Glue on wings, tail, and crown. A hole may be punched so that the bird can be hung.

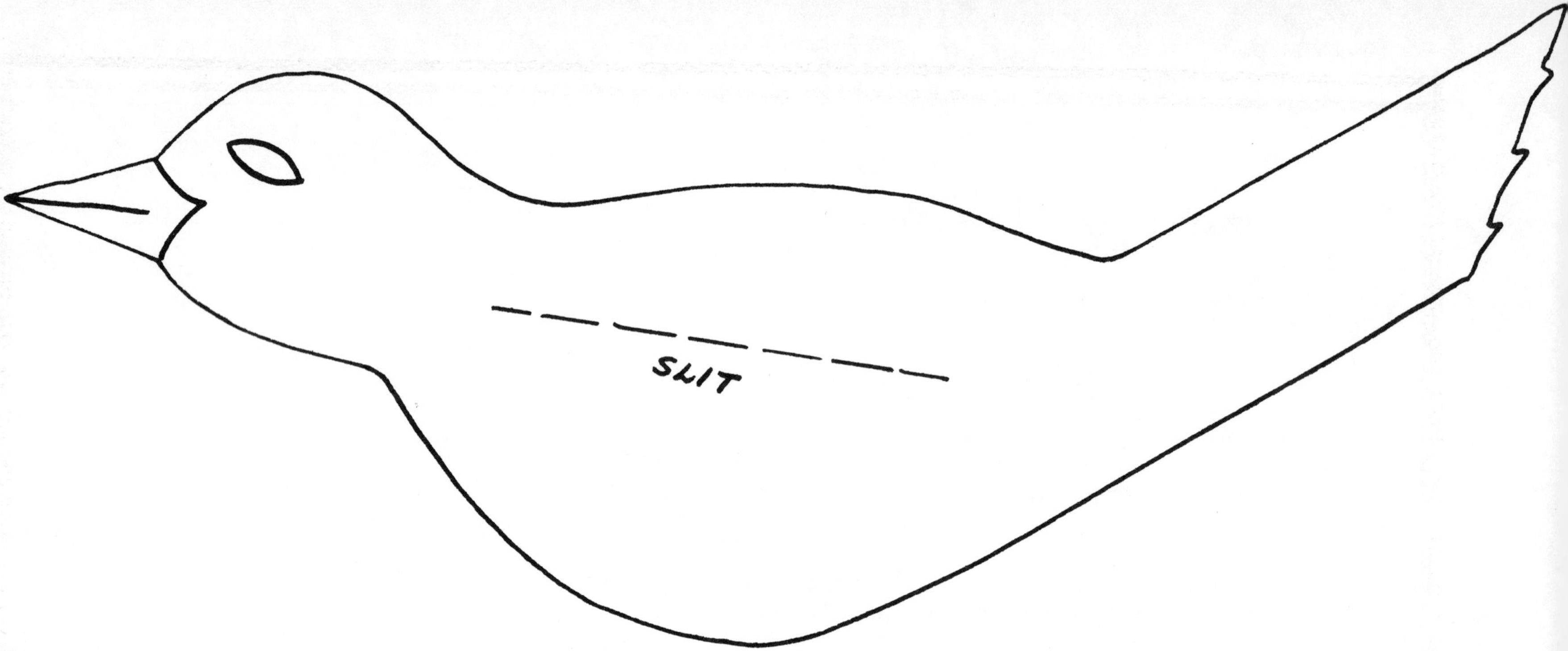
SLIT

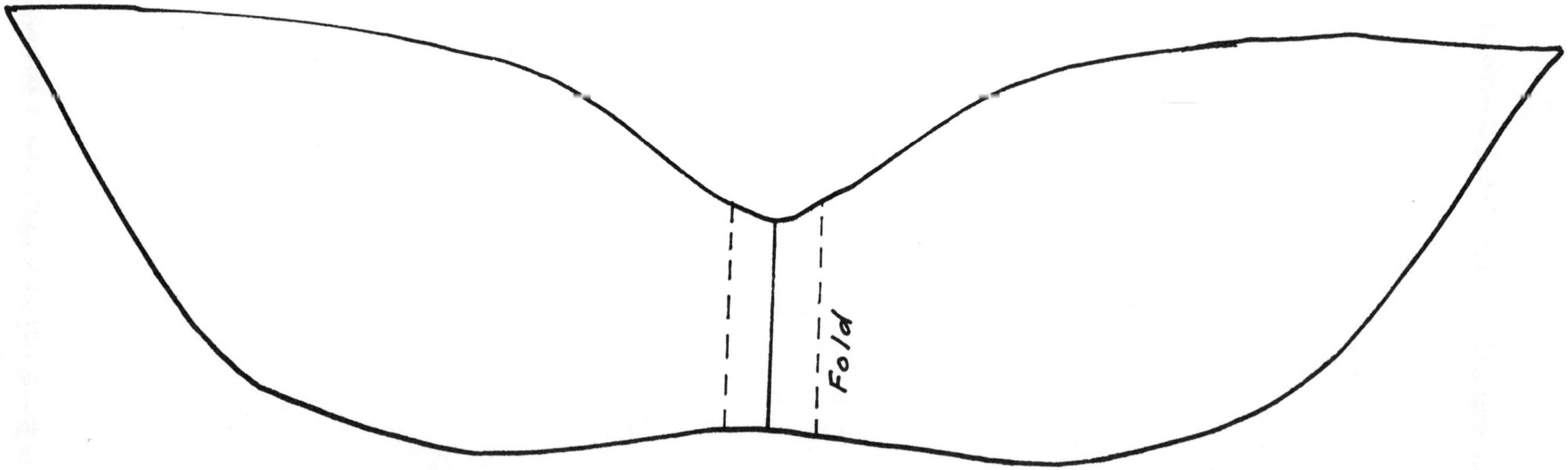
Fold

SUBJECT:	ELIJAH
ART ACTIVITY:	Paper-folded raven
MATERIALS:	Black paper for origami (there is a special paper sold for this purpose in school supply houses).
TEACHER PREPARATION:	Cut paper into 4" or 6" squares.
DIRECTIONS:	See illustrated step-by-step directions.

1. Fold a square of paper in half diagonally.

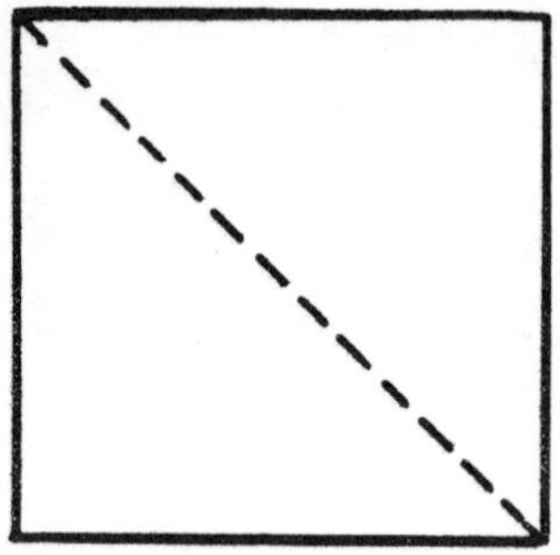

2. Fold this triangle in half. Crease.

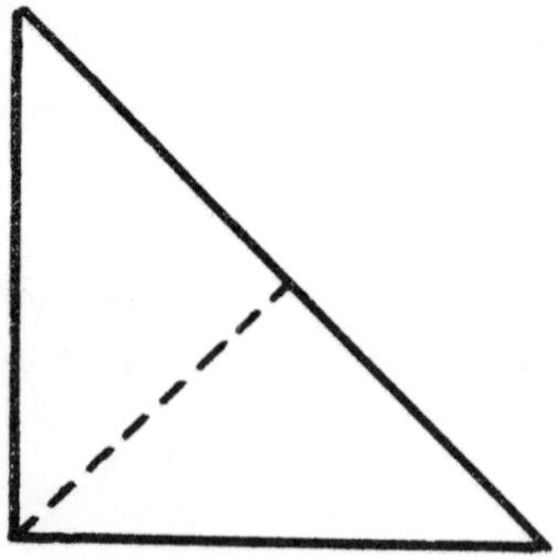

3. Fold this triangle in half. Crease.

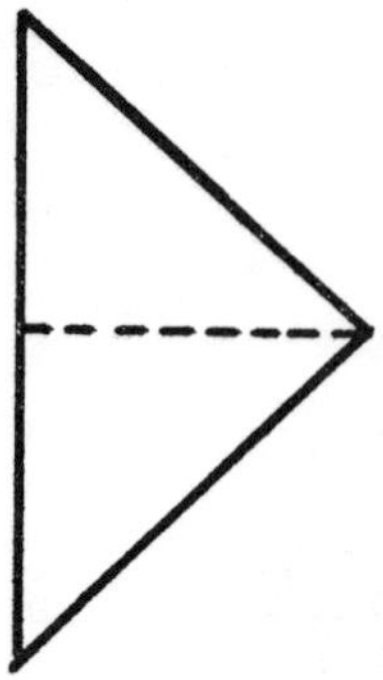

4. Unfold to largest triangle. Fold as indicated and crease.

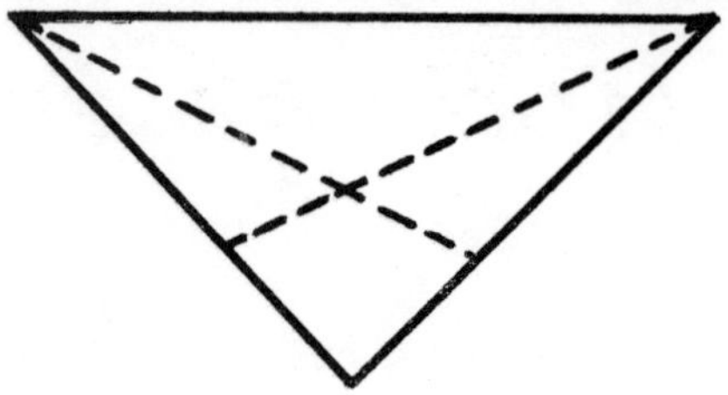

5. Unfold to largest triangle again. Fold.

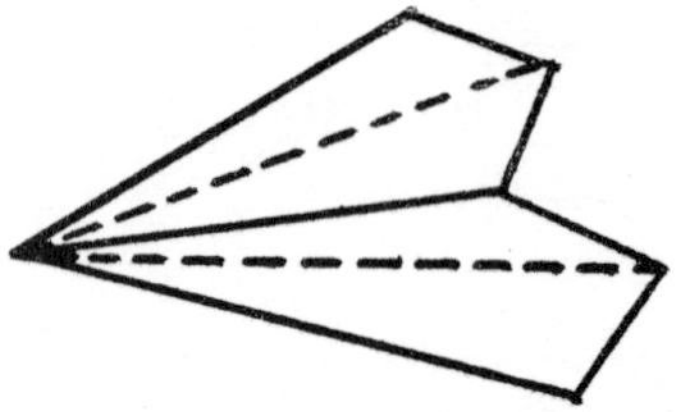

6. Unfold to largest triangle and pinch "wings" together as shown.

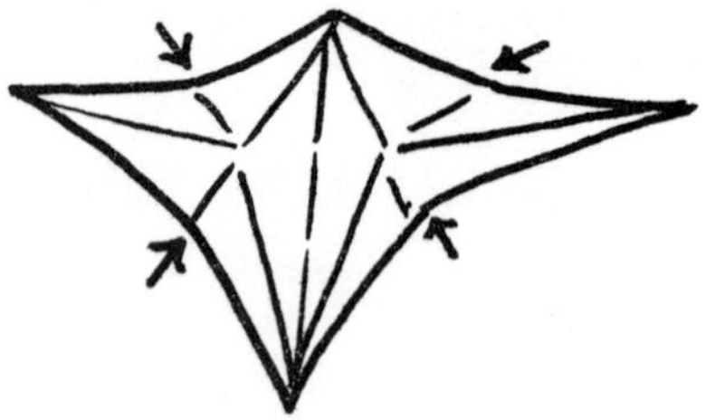

7. With closed fold on top, push longest tip in and fold down to form head. Fold back wing up and front wing down. Make eyes of cut paper.

In Elijah's time, pottery was used for many things. Can you find the match for each of these containers mentioned in the story of Elijah?

The widow of Zarephath brought Elijah a drink.

At home she had a small jar of oil.

The angel left a jar of water for Elijah.

Elijah anointed Hazael king of Syria.

Elisha used a jar of salt to sweeten the water.

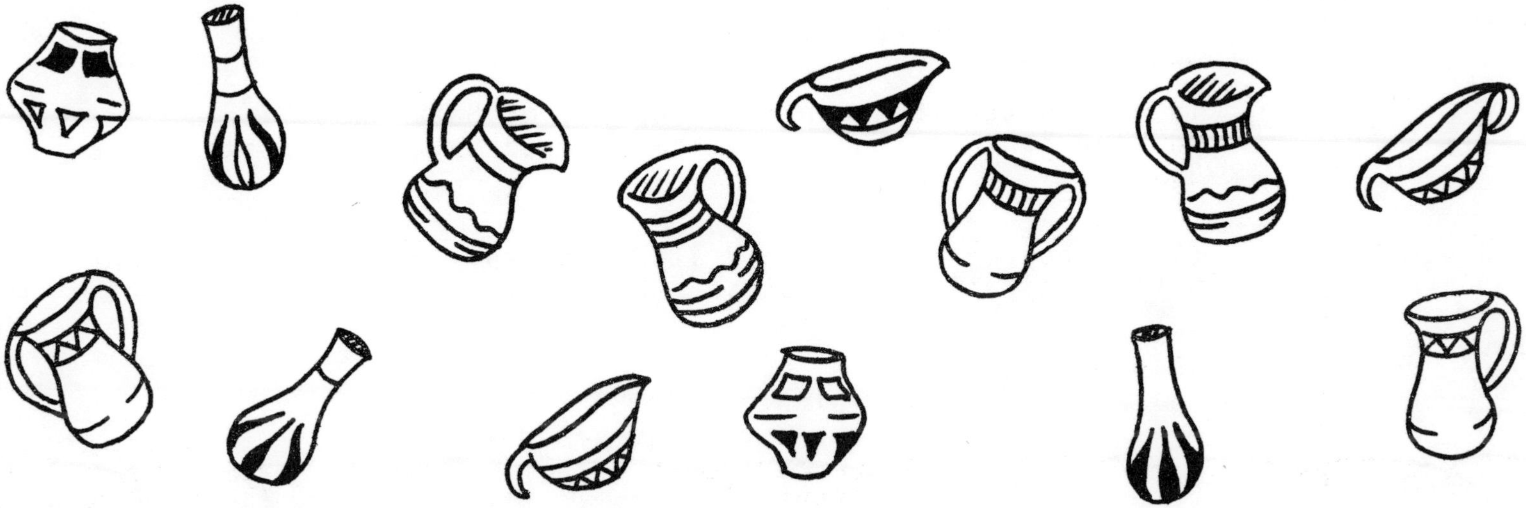

Write "True" or "False" beside each statement.

1. _____ Jezebel was a worshiper of the true God.

2. _____ Jezebel treated Elijah very kindly.

3. _____ Jezebel's husband was king of Egypt.

4. _____ Ahab was Jezebel's husband.

5. _____ Ravens brought food to Elijah while he was at the brook.

6. _____ The widow of Zarephath had plenty of food for Elijah.

7. _____ The widow's son was raised from death to life.

8. _____ In the contest between the prophets of Baal and Elijah, no fire consumed the sacrifice offered by the prophets of Baal.

9. _____ Elijah poured water on his altar to prove that his God could perform miracles regardless of circumstances.

10. _____ Ahab killed Elijah.

Can you find words here that are in the stories of Elijah? Listed on both sides are the words you are to find. Go up, down, sideways, or diagonally!

	C	I	S	R	D	R	A	Y	E	N	I	V	
	H	N	A	B	O	T	H	U	R	X	Y	L	
	A	I	C	Z	R	S	T	V	I	W	E	Z	
Sacrifice	R	A	R	A	V	E	N	S	F	M	T	K	Ahab
Ravens	I	R	I	R	P	L	M	B	R	S	P	L	Naboth
Bullocks	O	K	F	E	L	I	J	A	H	A	O	M	Vineyard
Obadiah	T	J	I	P	O	S	C	O	K	I	N	G	Jezreel
Elisha	H	L	C	H	I	H	G	F	D	S	E	S	Chariot
Zarephath	Z	A	E	A	Y	A	R	P	Y	R	E	K	Fire
Elijah	M	A	W	T	L	F	W	K	V	A	U	C	King
Carmel	A	B	A	H	A	E	H	O	T	E	Q	O	Queen
Israel	C	R	T	B	L	M	B	C	D	L	N	L	Rain
Baal	L	E	E	R	Z	E	J	E	R	I	M	L	Pray
	O	B	A	D	I	A	H	V	W	E	H	U	
	Q	M	A	S	F	C	L	O	M	S	J	B	

SUBJECT: ESTHER

BIBLE REFERENCES: Esther (entire book)

LEARNING GAME: Esther's Adventures

Materials: Old gameboard, heavy posterboard, or cardboard, felt pens, posterboard in contrasting color, one die, player pieces (buttons, cardboard squares, etc.), scorecard for each player

Construction: Make board as illustrated. Then cut 10, 2" x 3" cards from colored posterboard for the Activity cards. Write each of the following on a card:

1. Two guards plotted to assassinate the king. Move back 3 spaces.
2. Mordecai revealed the plot of the guards to Esther. Move forward 2.
3. All officials were required to bow before the king. Move back 3 spaces.
4. The king asked Haman how Mordecai should be honored for protecting the king's life. Move forward 2.
5. Haman was utterly humiliated after leading Mordecai through the city. Move back 1.
6. Haman promised to pay $20,000 into the king's treasury for the destruction of the Jews. Move back 3.

7. When Mordecai learned of Haman's plot he went out in the city and cried. Move forward 1.
8. When Mordecai was made Prime Minister, the Jews rejoiced. Move forward 3.
9. Many people pretended to be Jews when Mordecai was promoted for fear of what the Jews would do to them. Move back 2.
10. Purim is celebrated even today. Move forward 1.

DIRECTIONS FOR PLAYING:

This game may be played by 2 to 4 children. The die is rolled by each and the one who rolls the highest number begins the play. He rolls again and moves his playing piece the proper number of spaces on the board. If the space on which he lands has a plus or minus value, he records it on his score card. If the space has instructions to draw an activity card, the child will follow the instructions on the activity card and take the score of the space on which he finally lands. The player on his left then plays. As a player nears the end of the board, he may roll the exact number or any higher number to reach the end of the board. The game is over when every player has moved around the board. The player having the highest score wins.

(NOT ACTUAL SIZE)

Esther's Adventures
START
King Ahasuerus gave a big party +3
Queen Vashti refused to see king -4
Queen Vashti banished from kingdom -2
King Ahasuerus was most impressed with Esther +5
Esther told no one she was a Jew. +
Choose an Activity Card
Haman didn't know Esther was a Jew. -3
Mordecai refused to bow before Haman. +5
Haman plotted to kill all Jews. -4
Haman had gallows built for Jews -4
Mordecai put on sackcloth and ashes -2
The Jews fasted for Esther +6
Choose an Activity Card.
Esther invited Haman and king to a banquet -3
Haman ordered to lead Mordecai. +5
Esther revealed Haman's plot to king. +5
King reversed order to kill all Jews. +5
King ordered Haman hung. +5
Haman's ten sons were hanged. +5
Choose an Activity Card
Mordecai became prime minister. +3
Purim feast in honor of Esther. +1
The End
Activity Cards

SUBJECT:	ESTHER
ART ACTIVITY:	Plaster painting
MATERIALS:	For about 30 children you will need:

1 qt. white glue
1/4 cup dry plaster of paris
1/2 cup powdered tempera
Squeeze-type plastic bottles (such as catsup dispensers, detergent bottles, etc.)
30 pieces heavy cardboard or plywood
Tempera paints of different colors
Paint brushes

TEACHER PREPARATION: Add powdered tempera and plaster of paris to glue and mix well. Pour in squeeze containers.

DIRECTIONS: Have children sketch a very large Star of David on their board. Younger children may need a pattern. Then have them squeeze plaster mix over the lines of their sketch. Allow to dry thoroughly. They may then fill in areas of picture and background with paint, covering entire board.

*For 15 children try
2 cups white glue
4 t. dry wheat (wallpaper) paste
4 t. powdered tempera

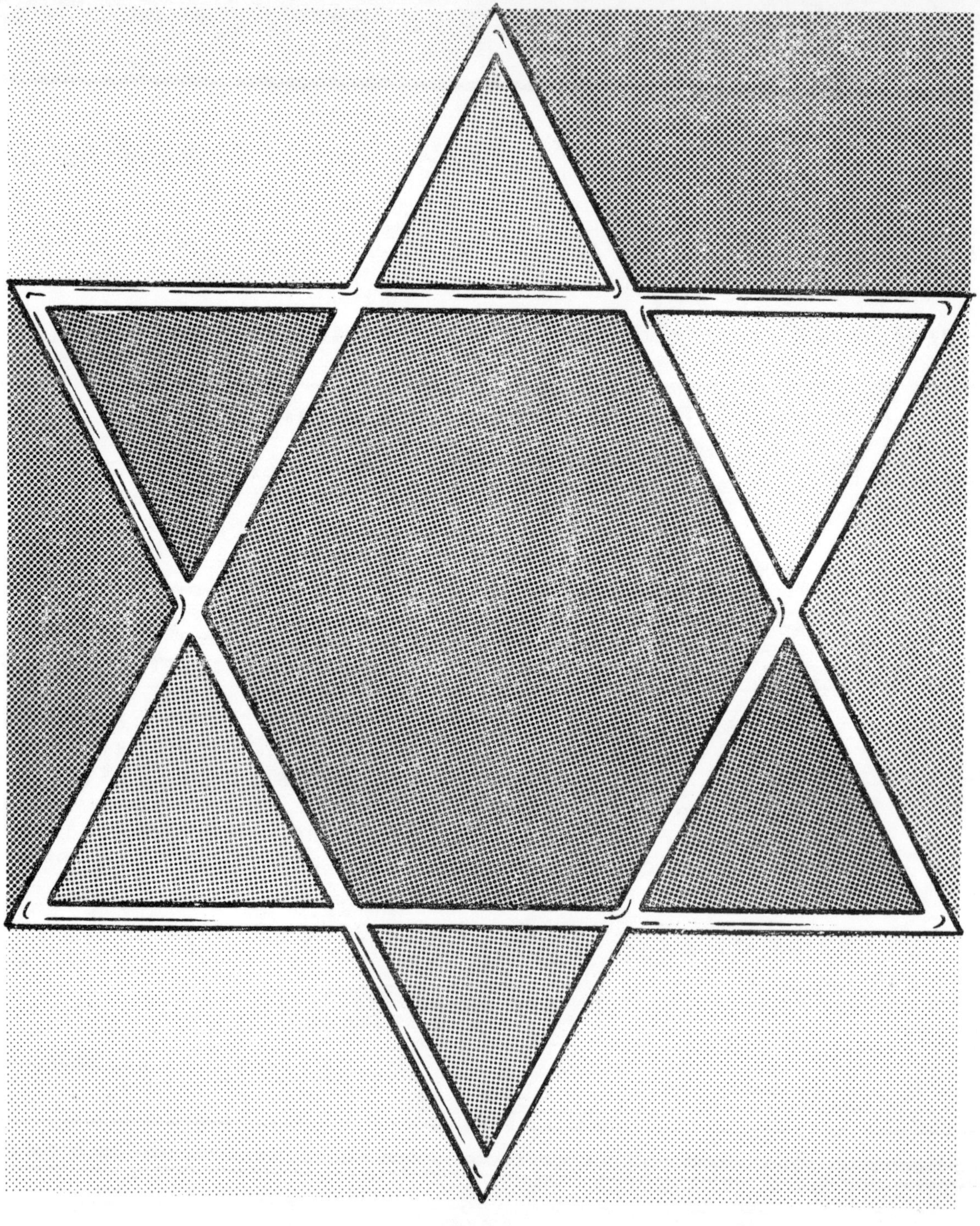

The Star of David became a worldwide symbol for the Jews. Color in all of the triangles below and you will find this star.

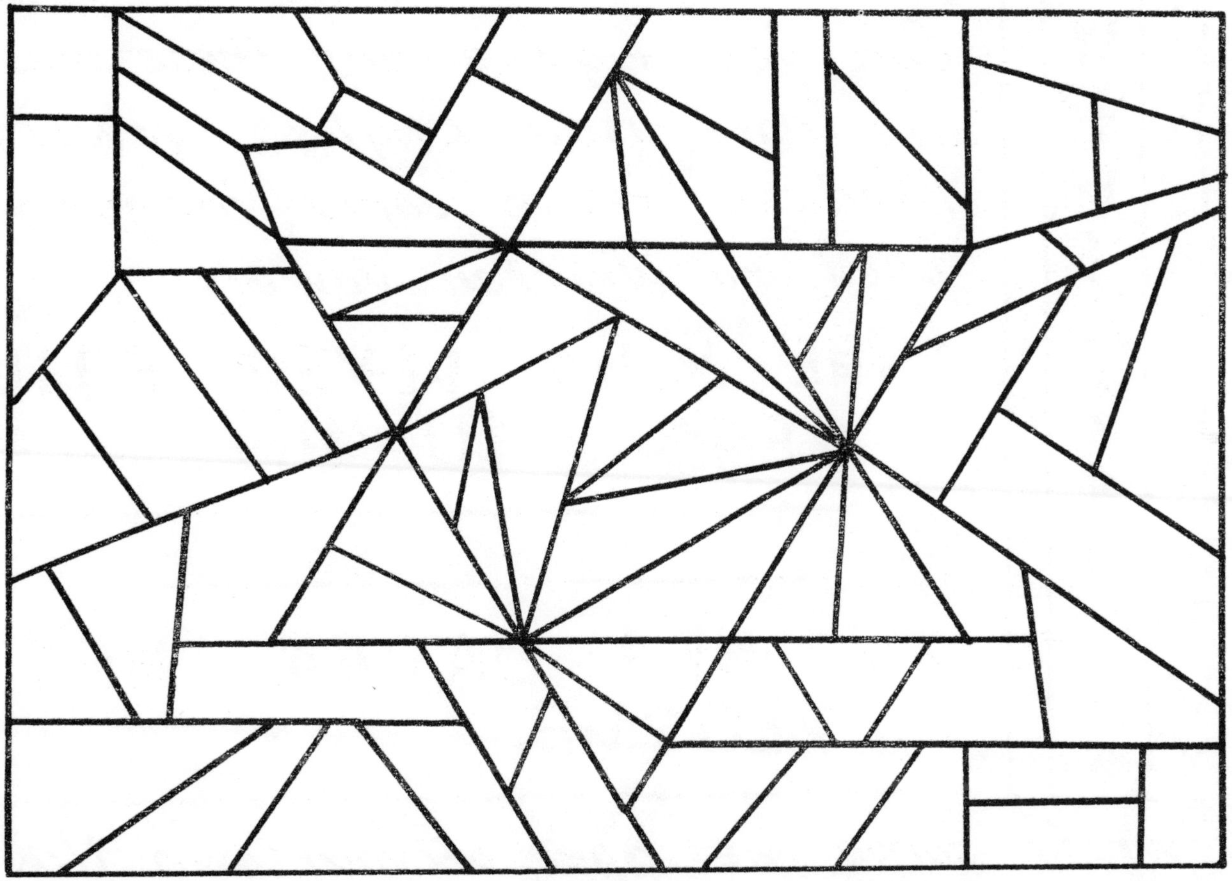

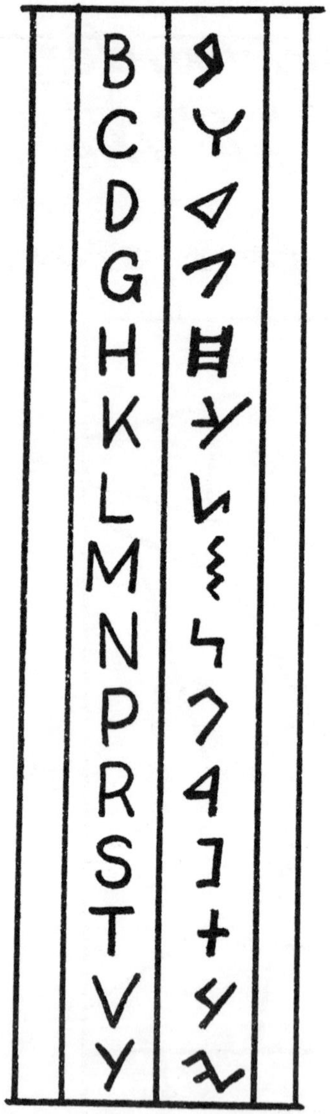

We can use symbols similar to those used by the Canaanites, Philistines and Hebrews 3000 years ago as a kind of code. Can you figure out these messages? We have used English vowels because these early languages used no written vowels.

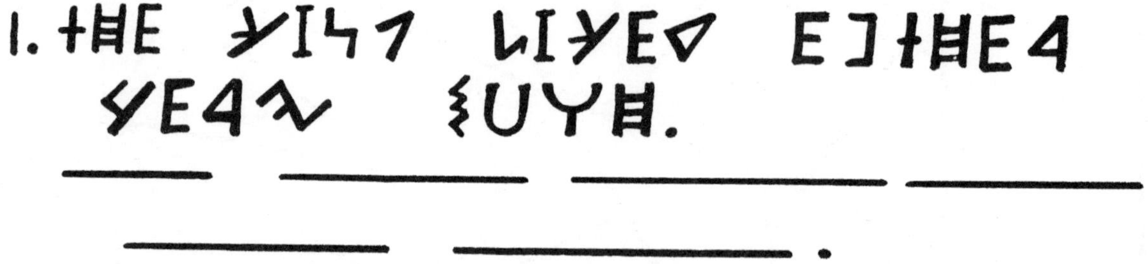

Now write some messages of your own. Use English letters when there are no code equivalents.

Write the fraction of the word indicated on the line next to each word. Then spell out the message on the line below.

$\frac{1}{3}$ of eat ____

$\frac{2}{5}$ of stood ____

$\frac{3}{4}$ of hero ____

$\frac{1}{4}$ of have ____

$\frac{1}{7}$ of evening ____

$\frac{1}{4}$ of lake ____

$\frac{1}{4}$ of pray ____

$\frac{2}{4}$ of Eden ____

$\frac{2}{4}$ of sail ____

$\frac{1}{7}$ of victory ____

$\frac{1}{3}$ of eve ____

$\frac{2}{5}$ of there ____

$\frac{1}{3}$ of ear ____

$\frac{1}{3}$ of jar ____

$\frac{1}{4}$ of even ____

$\frac{1}{3}$ of war ____

$\frac{1}{3}$ of sun ____

_ _ _ _ _ _   _ _ _ _ _ _   _ _ _ _   _ _ _

_ _ _ _.

SUBJECT:	DANIEL
BIBLE REFERENCES:	Daniel (entire book)
LEARNING GAME:	Concentrating on Daniel
Materials:	Two cardboard pieces, 13½" x 17½", exacto knife, solid color contact paper, tagboard, felt pens
Construction:	Cover one side of both cardboard pieces with contact paper. Then cut 20 windows in one of the cardboard pieces. The windows should measure approximately 2" x 3½" each, four windows across and five down. The windows are ½" from the edge and 1" between them. Glue the cutout cardboard onto the other board. This will make slots in which to place cards thus preventing them from slipping out of position. Cut tagboard into 20, 3¼" x 1-3/4" cards. Write questions pertaining to the story on 10 of the cards. Write answers to the questions on the other 10.
DIRECTIONS FOR PLAYING:	Two or more can play. Cards are turned face down on the board. The first player turns a card over and gives the answer. If the answer is correct, a second card is turned up. If that card is the answer to the first card turned up, the player gets to keep both cards. If an incorrect answer is given to the first card turned over, the player does not get to turn over a second card. The one with the most cards, when all cards are taken, wins.

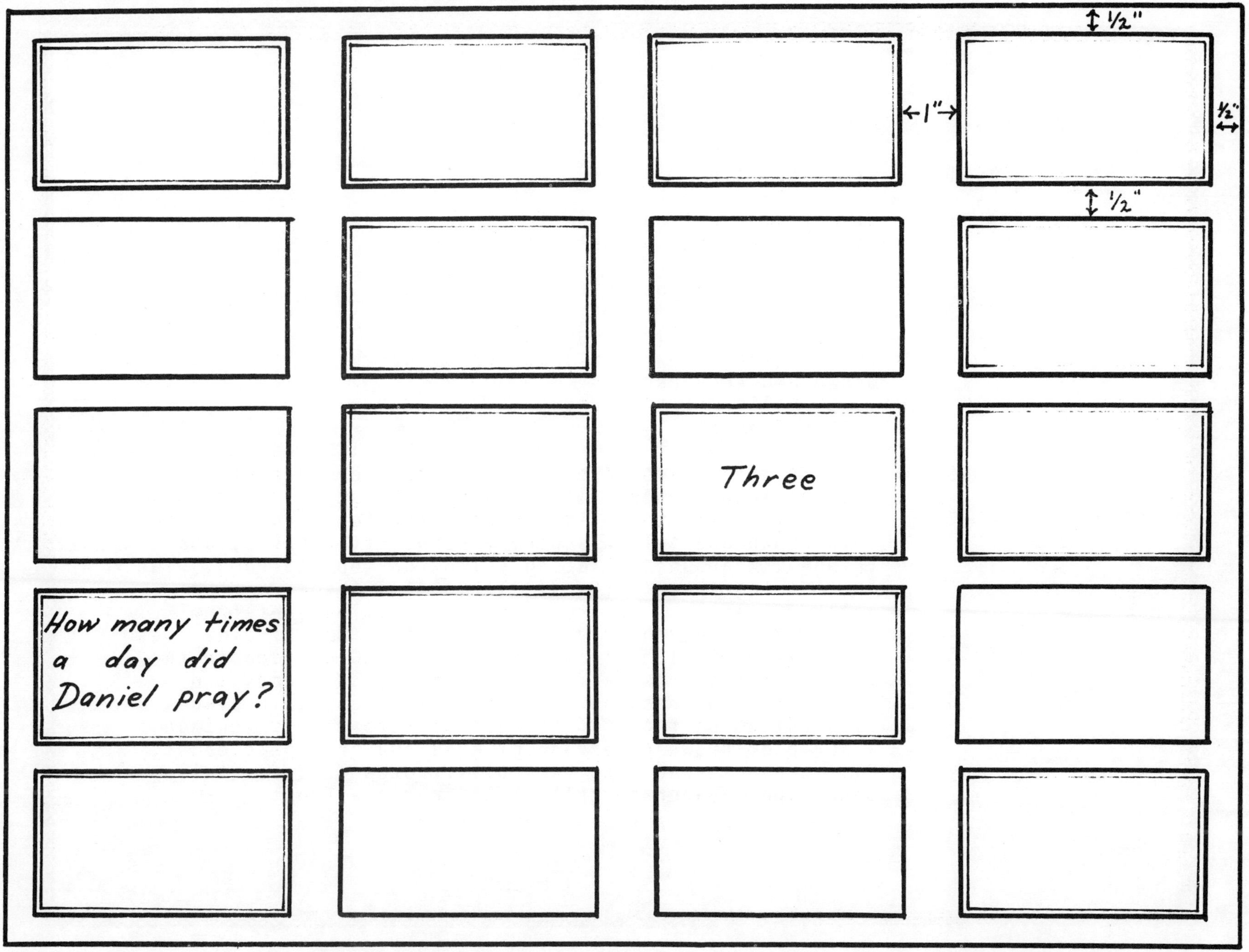
½"
←1"→
½"
½"
Three
How many times a day did Daniel pray?

SUBJECT: DANIEL

ART ACTIVITY: Paper cup lion

MATERIALS: Styrofoam paper cups, yellow pipe cleaners, brown, yellow, and green construction paper, scissors, glue

TEACHER PREPARATION: Provide the following for each child:

1, 4" square yellow construction paper
1, 4" square brown construction paper
Brown and green scraps
1, 5" yellow pipe cleaner
2 styrofoam cups

DIRECTIONS: Cut off the base of one styrofoam cup for face of lion. Leaving approximately 1" between, cut out 1" square pieces from the top of the other styrofoam cup. Holding both brown and yellow squares, round off corners, and fringe all around. Placing yellow on top of brown, glue the two together in the middle. Cut off some of the yellow fringe so the brown shows. Cut features from scraps and glue on previously-cut styrofoam circle. Cut a ½" piece of pipe cleaner for mouth. Glue face in the middle of the brown and yellow pieces. Cut ears and glue onto construction paper in the appropriate places. Glue bottom part of fringe onto styrofoam cup. Fringe a scrap of brown paper and glue on end of pipe cleaner. Glue pipe cleaner onto back of styrofoam cup for tail. Bend pipe cleaner so tail shows from the front.

FRONT

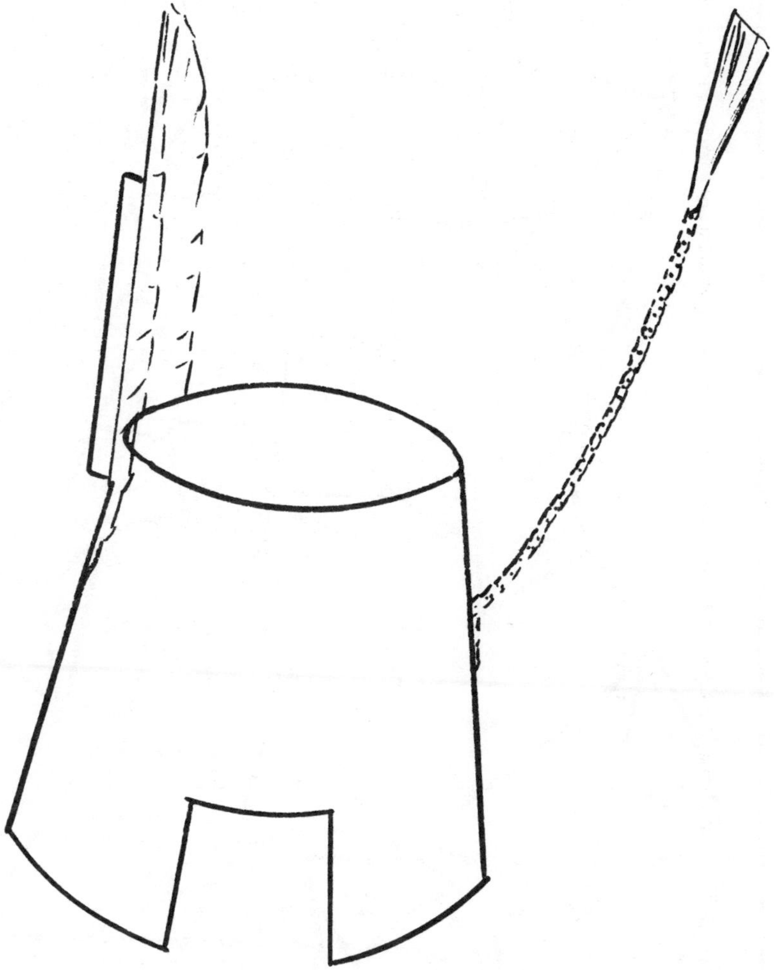

SIDE

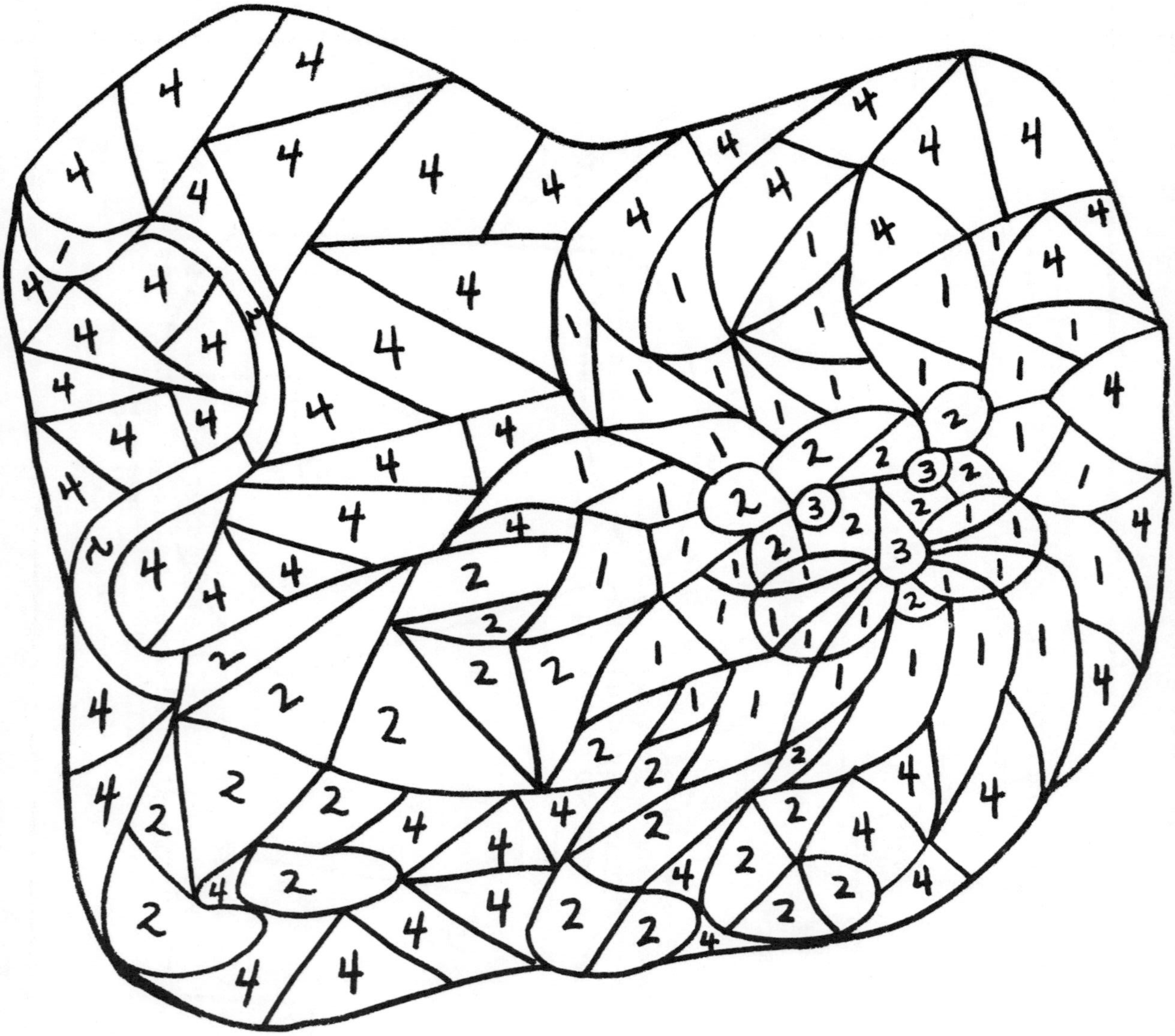

Daniel was thrown into the lions' den. To find a picture of the lion, fill in the numbered sections with the right colors.

1 = YELLOW 2 = ORANGE 3 = BLACK 4 = BROWN

Circle the correct ending for the paragraph. Read Daniel 2 for clues.

1. King Nebuchadnezzar chose three young men to be trained to become leaders in Babylon. They had to learn the language and even had to change their names to Babylonian names. The three boys were:

   Peter, James and John
   Shadrach, Meshach and Abednego
   Esau, Jacob and Isaac

2. One night King Nebuchadnezzar had a very strange dream that greatly bothered him. But then he found he could not remember the dream. So he called all his wise men but they could not tell him his dream. When Daniel heard this, he went to the king and said he would try but asked for:

   the Bible which would help him
   his three friends to help him
   a little time

3. After Daniel interpreted the King's dream, Nebuchadnezzar actually seemed to believe in the one true God of Israel. But he changed his mind very rapidly. He ordered his men to:

   kill all those who believed in God
   build a statue of himself and order all to worship it
   throw all those who believed in God in the lions' den

Move from square to square--up, down, from side to side, but <u>not</u> diagonally--to find the hidden sentence in the diagram. Start with D.

W	L	E	I	D
A	S	T	N	A
H	T	H	R	O
E	O	T	N	W
L	N	S	I	N
I	O	D	E	N

Do not cross any lines. Use each block only once.

SUBJECT:	JONAH
BIBLE REFERENCES:	Jonah (entire book)
LEARNING GAME:	Make Your Own Puzzle
Materials:	An appealing picture, scissors, felt pens, two pieces of tagboard, glue
Construction:	First glue the picture on tagboard; then cut the picture into large pieces, making sure the pieces do not get mixed (otherwise you might spend a lot of time putting them back together again!). Draw an outline of each shape on the tagboard. Write questions on the shapes on the board and the answers on the corresponding pieces of the puzzle.
DIRECTIONS FOR PLAYING:	The child tries to put the picture together by matching the items.

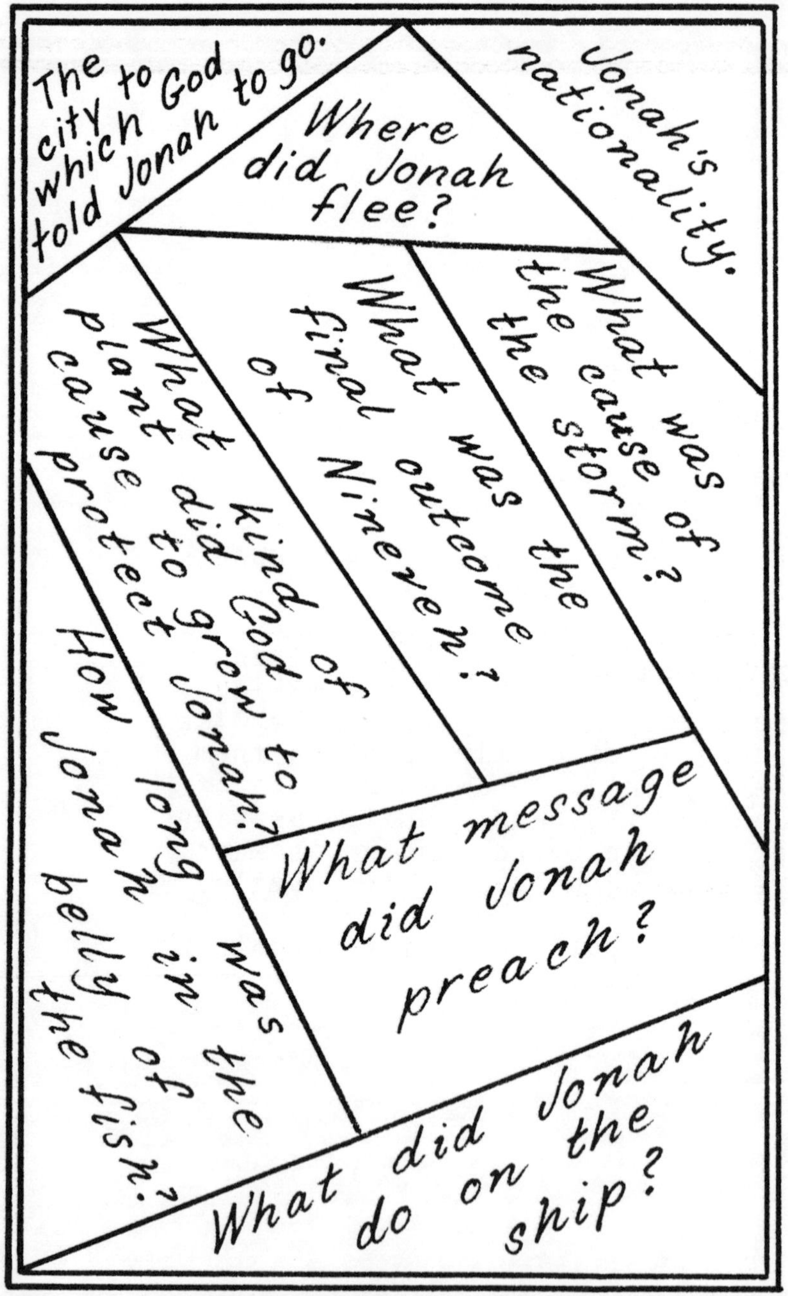

The city to which God told Jonah to go.
Where did Jonah flee?
Jonah's nationality.
What was the final outcome of Nineveh?
What was the cause of the storm?
What kind of plant did God cause to grow to protect Jonah?
How long was Jonah in the belly of the fish?
What message did Jonah preach?
What did Jonah do on the ship?

TAGBOARD FRAME

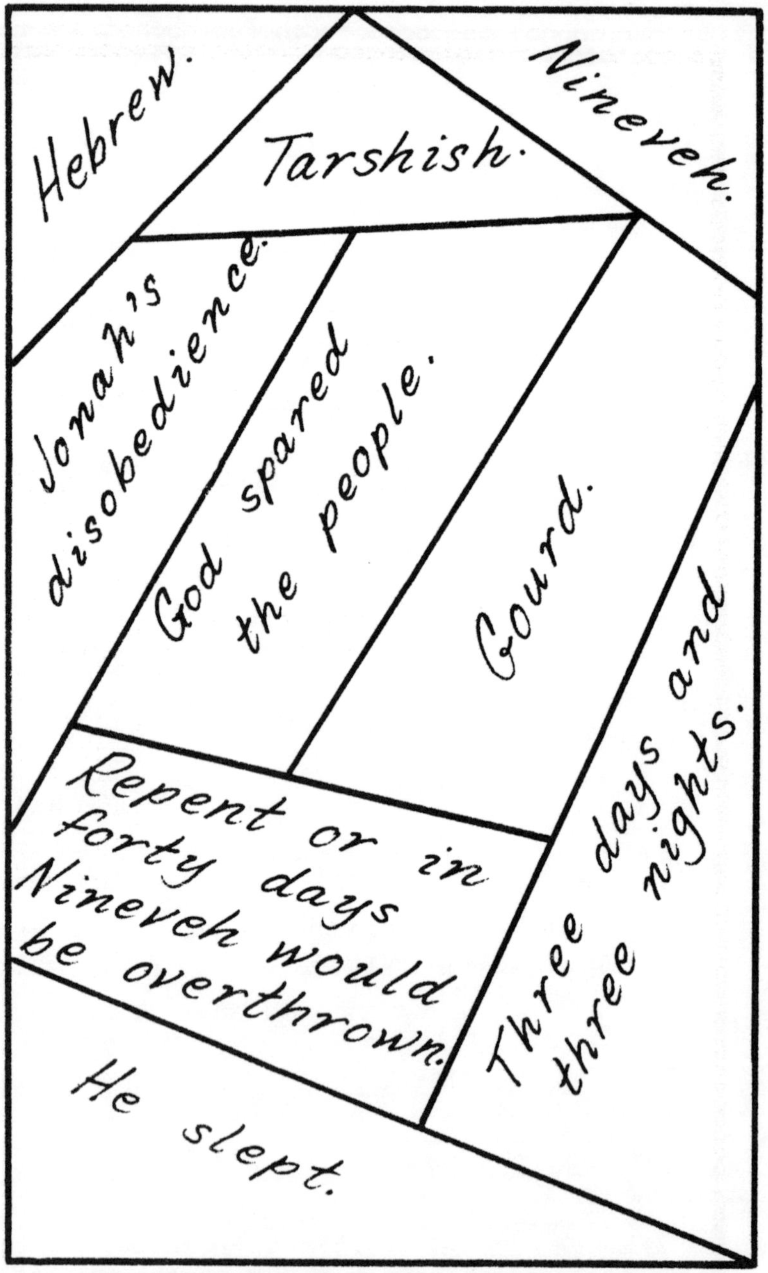

Hebrew.
Tarshish.
Nineveh.
Jonah's disobedience.
God spared the people.
Gourd.
Three days and three nights.
Repent or in forty days Nineveh would be overthrown.
He slept.

BACK OF PICTURE

SUBJECT:	JONAH
ART ACTIVITY:	Stuffed sea animals
MATERIALS:	Newspaper, tagboard, tempera, paint brushes, scissors, stapler, paint, white butcher paper
TEACHER PREPARATION:	Make tagboard patterns of sea animals, if desired. Prepare paint and pour in bowls. Spread newspaper on tables.
DIRECTIONS:	Trace pattern of sea animal on butcher paper. Turn pattern over and trace the same. Paint both pieces. After they are dry, cut them out. Staple the edges of one side; stuff the insides with newspaper and staple the edges.

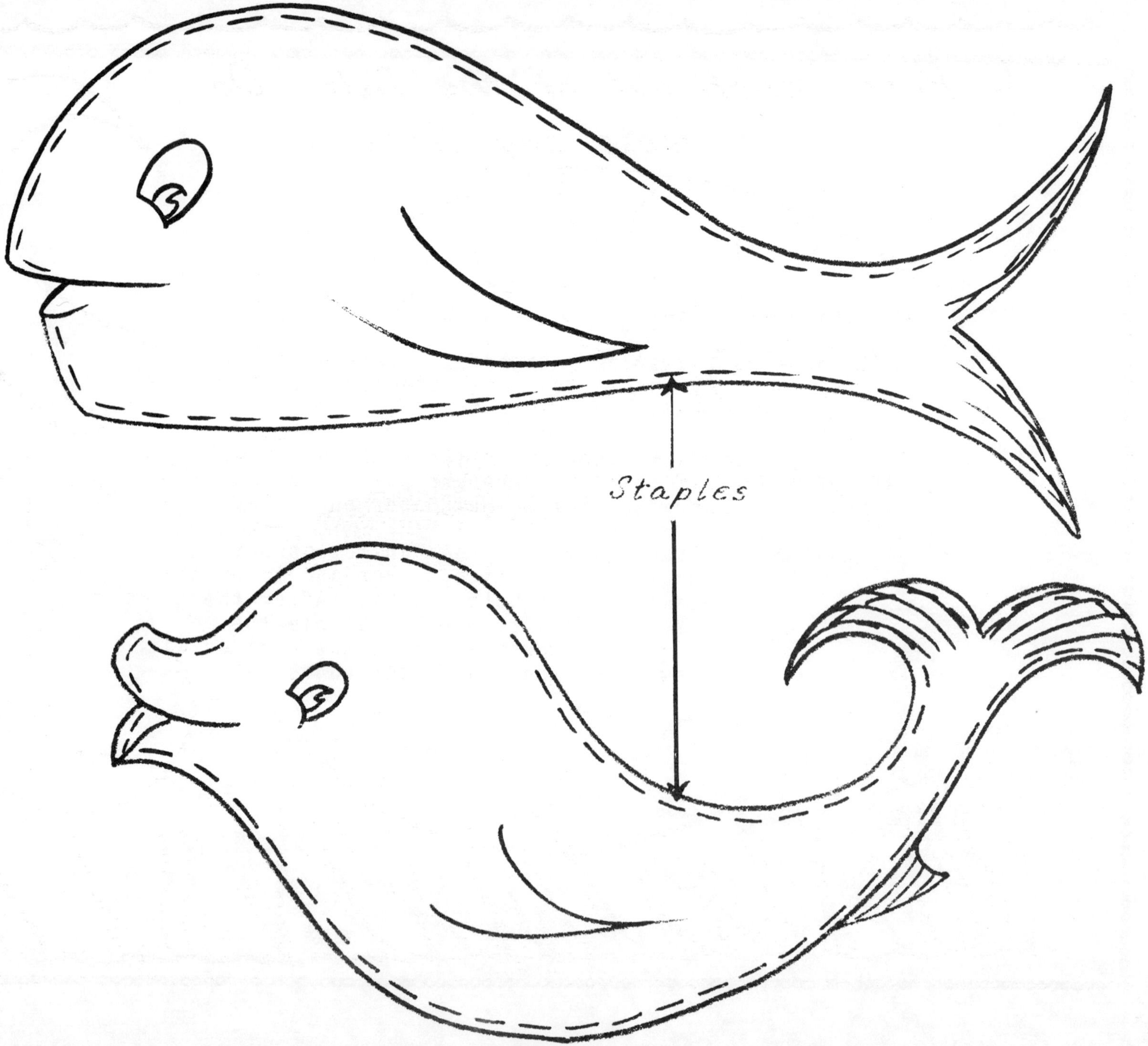
Staples

Help Jonah out of the fish. Do not cross any lines.

Read each paragraph and write the conclusion to each:

1. In the province of Galilee lived the prophet Jonah. He was a good man who often preached about judgment. The Lord decided to send him on a mission. What did God tell him? (Jonah 1:2)

2. Jonah was unwilling, however, to risk his life to save a few heathens so he decided instead to . . . (Jonah 1:3)

3. Finally, the men threw Jonah into the waters. But Jonah did not drown. As he sank below the waves, Jonah . . . (Jonah 1:17)

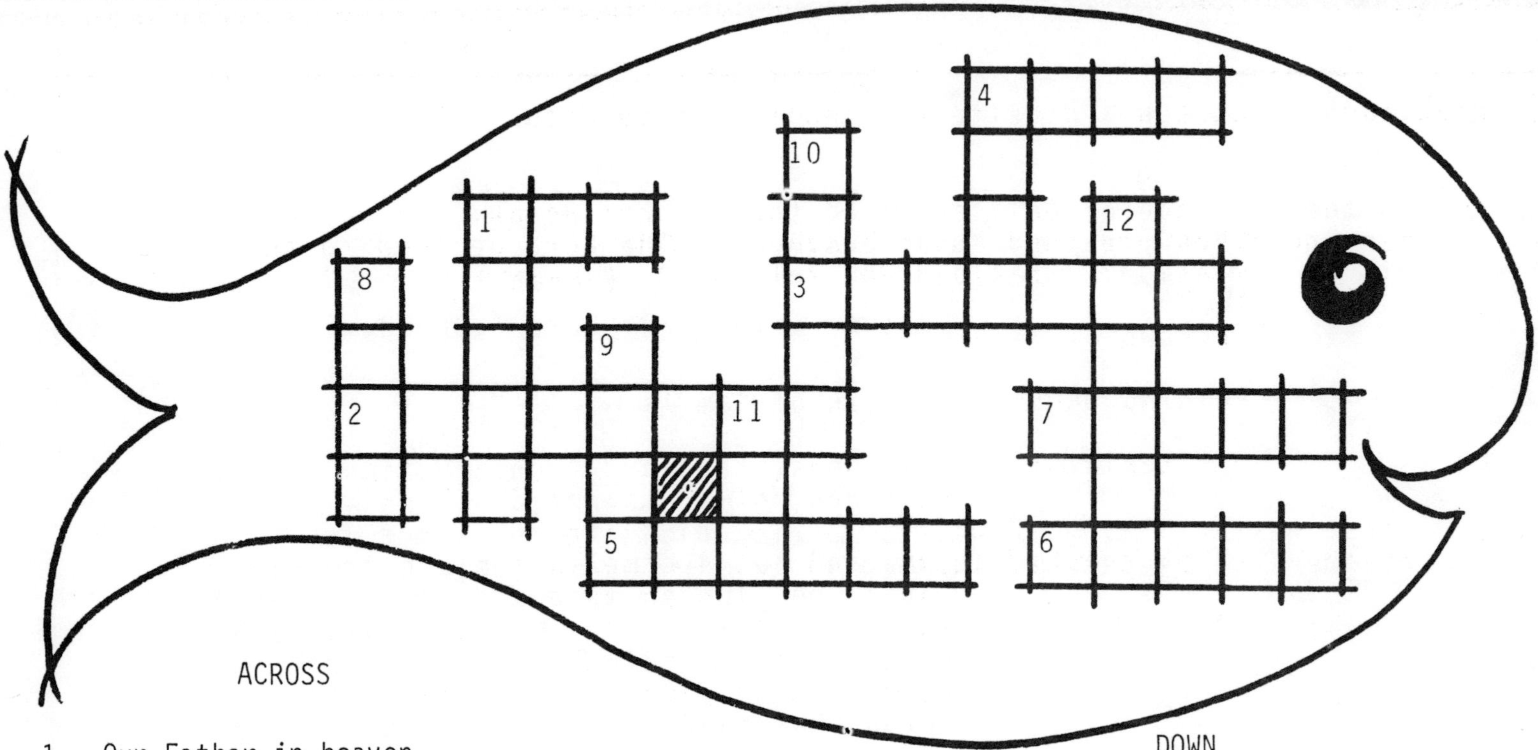

ACROSS

1. Our Father in heaven
2. Jonah took a ship going to this place. (1:3)
3. Jonah was sent to preach to this place. (1:2)
4. This swallowed Jonah. (1:17)
5. While he was inside an animal, Jonah _ _ _ _ _ _ _. (2:1)
6. While at sea, a _ _ _ _ _ arose. (1:4)
7. Part of the animal in which Jonah lived. (2:1)

DOWN

1. The plant that sheltered Jonah (4:6)
4. To run away.
8. Nineveh was a _ _ _ _. (1:2)
9. Jonah went to Joppa to find a _ _ _ _. (1:3)
10. The prophet of the story (1:1)
11. The sailors threw Jonah into the _ _ _. (1:15)
12. Jonah asked the people of Nineveh to _ _ _ _ _ _ _. (3:10)

SUBJECT:	THE BIRTH OF JESUS
BIBLE REFERENCES:	Matthew 1:18-2:23; Luke 1:26-38, 2:1-20
LEARNING GAME:	Caravan of Camels
Materials:	Felt pens, tagboard, construction paper, scissors, glue, magnetic strips
Construction:	Draw and cut 4 camels from construction paper and glue on tagboard (see pattern). Put 2 magnetic strips on each camel's hump. Draw and cut bundle-like shapes from construction paper. On these write words that make a verse or part of a verse. On the back of these word cards attach magnetic strips.
DIRECTIONS FOR PLAYING:	The child places the bundles on the camels in sequential order to make a verse.

I
bring
you
good
tidings
of
great
joy

SUBJECT:	THE BIRTH OF JESUS
ART ACTIVITY:	Angel with Q-Tips
MATERIALS:	Blue construction paper, Q-Tips, White crayons, felt pens (optional), glue
TEACHER PREPARATION:	You may want to have angels drawn on the construction paper for the very young children.
DIRECTIONS:	Have child draw the outline of an angel. Draw facial features and color the garment of angel. Glue Q-Tips on garment in any pattern desired.

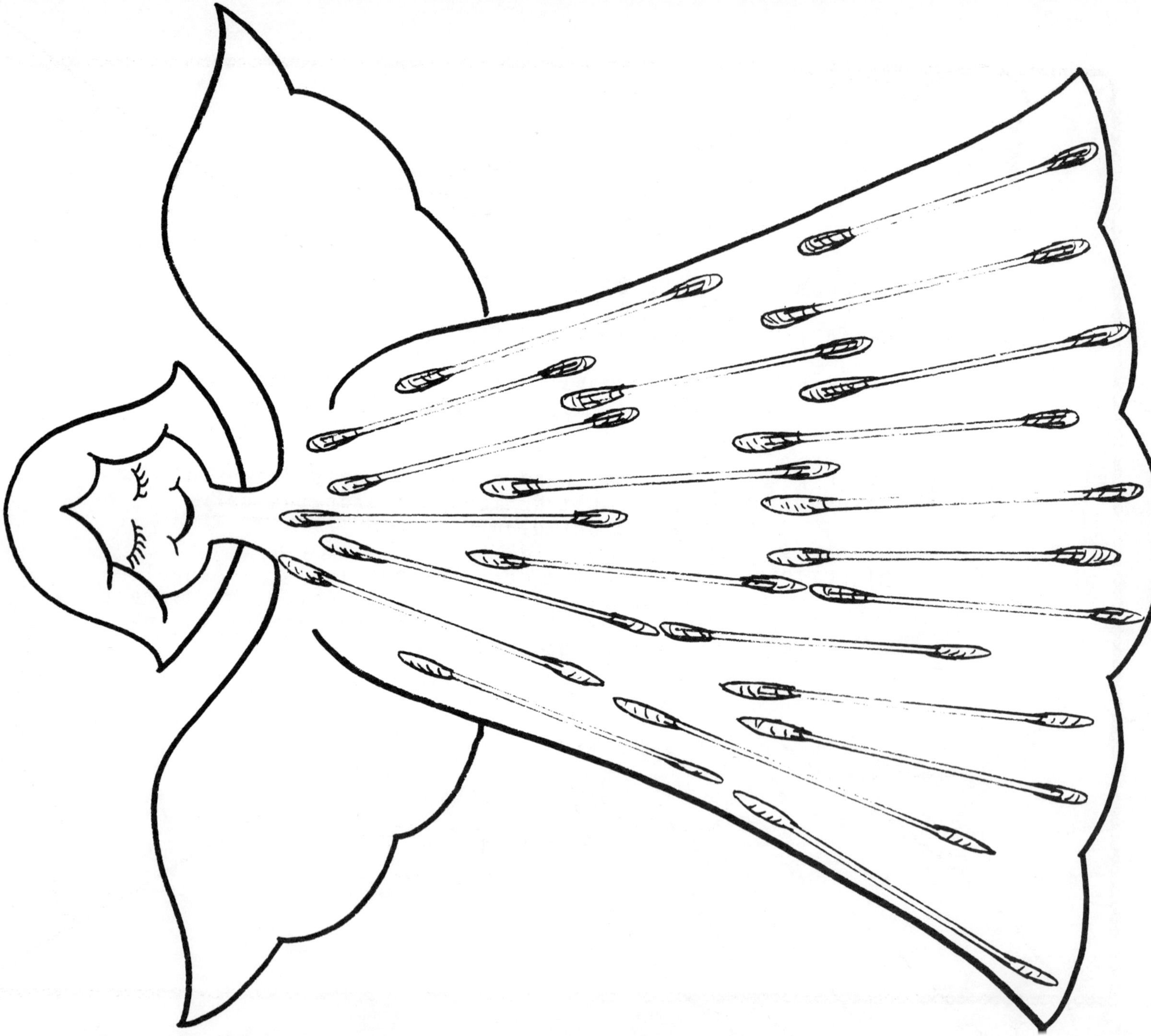

COLOR THE ANGEL

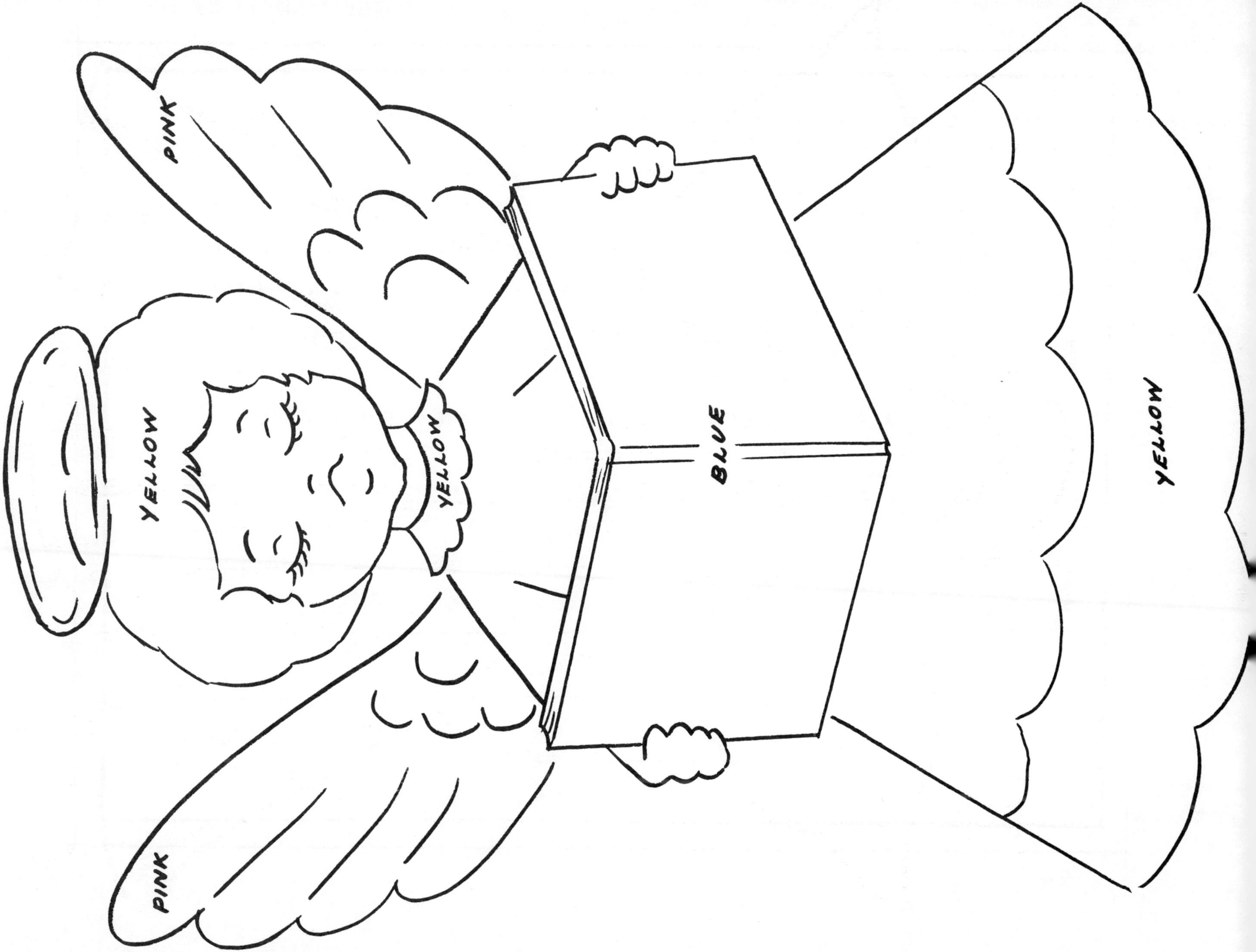

Find out what the verse says. Add or subtract the letters according to the directions. Then write your answer.

S A N D - S + S H E E P + S + H A L L - E P + B + R I N G + F + O R

+ T H E - E + A + S O U N D - U D, + H A N D - H + T H E - E + O U T

- T + S H E - E + A L T A R - A R + C + A L L + H + I S + N O N E

- O N E + A + M E + J E S U S: F + O R + H E M - M + S H E - E

+ A L L + S O M E - O M E + A V E + H E - E + I S + P E O + P A L

- A + E + F A R - A R + R O M + T H E + I R E - E + S + I N + S.

Solve these math problems to crack the secret code. Find that number underneath a blank and write the corresponding letter above it. Each time that number appears in the code, the same letter is written.

___   ___ ___ ___ ___ ___   ___ ___ ___   ___ ___ ___ ___   ___ ___ ___ ___ ___ ___ ___
16   49 35 16 81 18   20 8 56   18 8 8 72   54 16 72 16 81 18 48

___ ___   ___ ___ ___ ___ ___   ___ ___ ___.
8 40   18 35 12 30 54   36 8 20

A 5 X 6	B 7 X 7	D 8 X 9	E 4 X 3	F 5 X 8
G 6 X 3	I 4 X 4	J 6 X 6	N 9 X 9	O 4 X 2
R 5 X 7	S 6 X 8	T 9 X 6	U 7 X 8	Y 4 X 5

SUBJECT: PARABLES

BIBLE REFERENCES: See next page for listing of familiar parables

LEARNING GAME: Temple Write-in

Materials: Tagboard, exacto knife, felt pens

Construction: Cut tagboard into temple-like shape (see illustration). Cut evenly spaced windows. On the front, under each window, write the scrambled name of a parable. On the back, under each window, write the correct name of the parable, in the same order as on the front, so that the board can be flipped over to check answers.

DIRECTIONS FOR PLAYING: The child places his paper under the "temple" and writes through each cutout window the correct name of the parable that is written below the window. After completing the exercise, he flips the "temple" over and places it on top of his paper to check the answers.

PARABLES

The Sower (Matthew 13:1-23)

The Wedding Feast (Matthew 22:1-14)

The Ten Virgins (Matthew 25:1-13)

The Great Supper (Luke 14:7-24)

The Lost Sheep (Luke 15:1-7)

The Lost Coin (Luke 15:8-10)

The Prodigal Son (Luke 15:11-32)

Parable of the Pounds (Luke 19:11-27)

The Mustard Seed (Luke 13:18-19)

SODAARGOMNTAI
STWREEHO
SNDPGLROOIA
STCNLOOI
STTHLNTAEE
SWTDA GFDIENE
SLTSPHEOE
STNVNGRIEI
DBLVNDRAEEAEE

FRONT

GOOD SAMARITAN
THE SOWER
PRODIGAL SON
LOST COIN
THE TALENTS
WEDDING FEAST
LOST SHEEP
TEN VIRGINS
LEAVENED BREAD

BACK

SUBJECT: PARABLES

ART ACTIVITY: Glue art

MATERIALS: White construction paper, black spray paint (any kind), glue in squeeze bottles (each child will need one)

TEACHER PREPARATION: None. You will need to spray the glue drawings after they are completed. A well-ventilated area may be set aside where this can be done, and be sure to cover entire area with newspaper.

DIRECTIONS: Child can depict parable by "drawing" with his glue bottle. The lines need to be distinct and the drawing large. Small lines of glue tend to run into each other. Do not squeeze glue too close to the edge. Let dry. Then teacher can spray black paint lightly over the entire picture. The effect is that of a photograph.

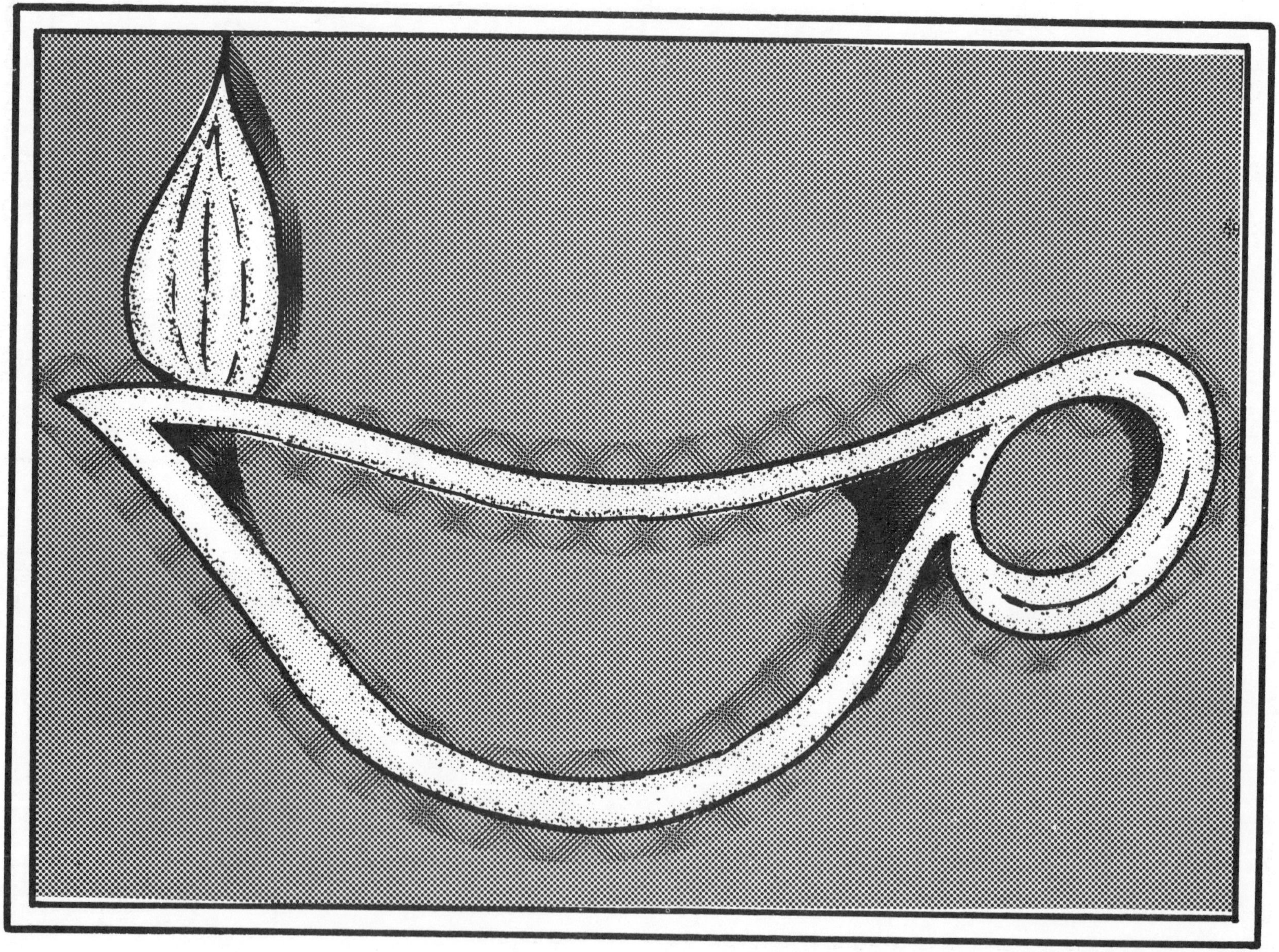

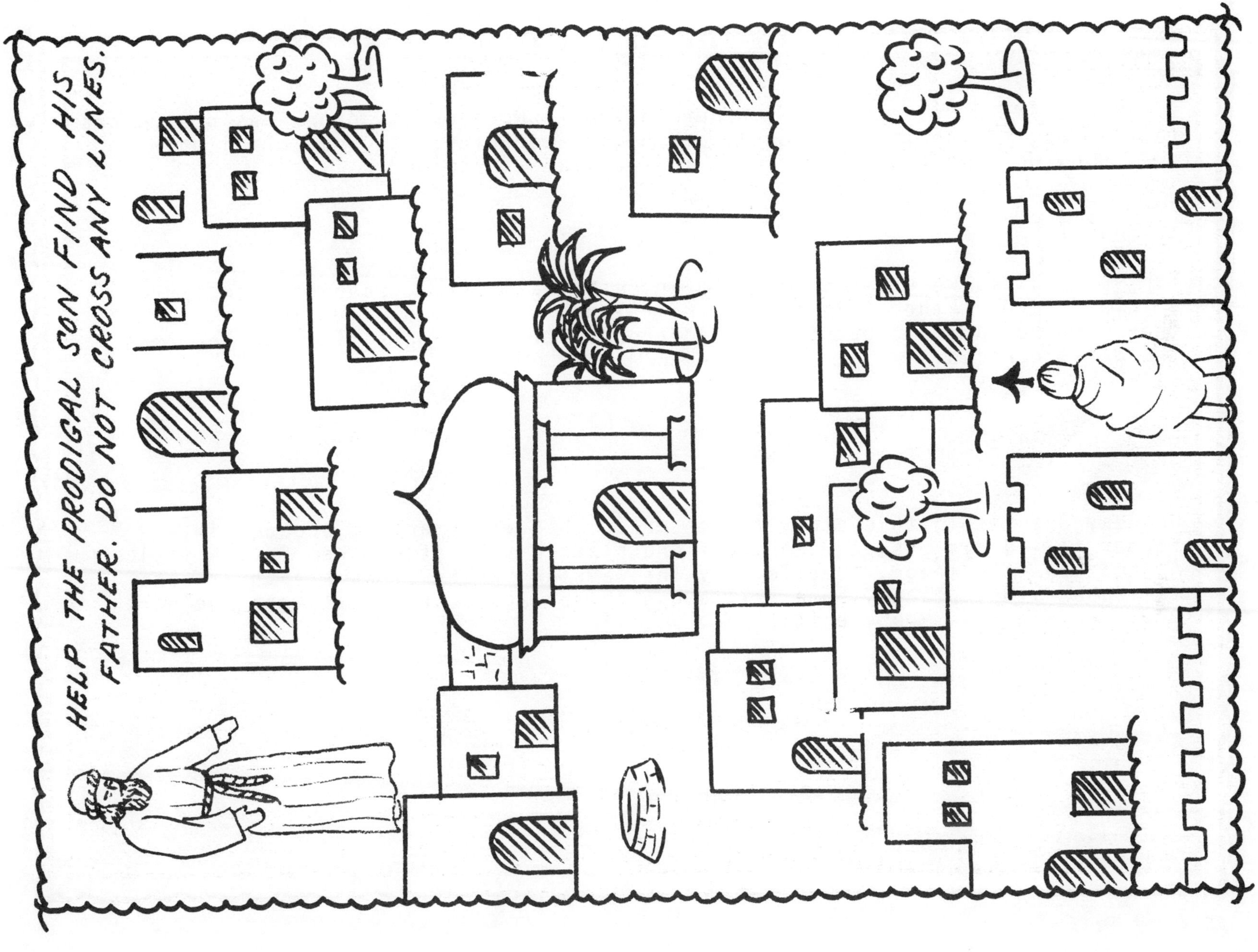
HELP THE PRODIGAL SON FIND HIS FATHER. DO NOT CROSS ANY LINES.

Read the stories and follow the directions at the end of each one.

I was one of 10 coins. But my owner lost me. However, my owner was determined to find me, so she lit her candle and began searching. She was thrilled when she found me. What do you think I looked like? Draw me.

Ten young girls were asked to accompany a bridal party. Each of them carried a lamp. Five of the girls filled their lamps with oil. Five did not, so they were not able to greet the bridegroom. Draw a lamp similar to the ones the girls carried.

One day Jesus told this story to the crowd that was standing around him. A farmer filled his basket with seeds and started to scatter them in the field. As he threw the seeds, some fell by the wayside, where birds ate them; some fell upon stony places, some fell among thorns and others fell into the earth. Draw the field as you see it.

You will need an extra sheet of paper and your Bible to work out your answers. Have fun!

1. Write upside down what the seed stands for in the parable of the sower. (Matt. 13:1-23)

2. With the hand you do not ordinarily use, write what Jesus compared to the mustard seed. (Luke 13:18-19)

3. The parable about a man who had two sons is known as the Parable of the ______________ ____________. Write your answer two lines tall. (Luke 15:11-32)

4. In the parable of the 10 coins, what kind of coins were they? Write your answer backwards. (Luke 15:8-10)

5. Write the book of the Bible in all capital letters in which the parable of the 100 sheep is found. (Luke 15:1-7)

6. Put the words in these sentences in correct order:

   a. ready teaches The us Ten be Virgins spiritually the Parable of to

   b. effective becomes describes Sower the of The God's Word Parable which in manner the

   c. forgiveness story of a is God's Son Prodigal Parable The of the

   d. sinners rejoicing God's Lost pictures us for Coin of the over repenting Parable The

   e. Feast Wedding salvation accept all it who for Parable The that teaches is of the

SUBJECT:	MIRACLES
BIBLE REFERENCES:	See the next page for listing of the more familiar miracles.
LEARNING GAME:	Miracle Match
Materials:	Construction paper, poster board, felt pens, tagboard, paper clips or brads, mystic tape, hole punch, contact paper
Construction:	Draw a ship on poster board (see illustration) with two masts. Poke holes on the masts where the hooks are to be placed. Twist paper clip and push one end through hole. The other side of the paper clip will need to be held with masking tape. Cover the back of the board with contact paper. Make cards to fit on the hooks. On half of the cards write the miracles performed, and on the rest of them write the corresponding names of those connected with those miracles.
DIRECTIONS FOR PLAYING:	The child takes the cards and matches the miracles with the correct people.

MIRACLES

Crossing the Red Sea (Exodus 13:20-15:21)
Water Made Sweet (Exodus 15:22-27)
Manna for the Israelites (Exodus 16:1-21)
Water from a Rock (Exodus 17:1-7)
The Budding of Aaron's Rod (Numbers 17)
Crossing the Jordan (Joshua 3-4)
The Walls of Jericho (Joshua 5:13-6:27)
The Sun and the Moon Stand Still (Joshua 10-11)
Naaman, the Leper (2 Kings 5:1-14)
The Story of Hezekiah (2 Kings 20)

Jesus Stills the Storm (Matthew 8:23-27)
Jesus Heals a Mad Man (Matthew 8:28-34)
Blind Man of Bethsaida Healed (Mark 8:22-26)
The Healing of the Paralytic (Luke 5:18-26)
Jesus Heals the Man with the Withered Hand (Luke 6:6-11)
Blind Bartimaeus Healed (Luke 18:35-43)
Healing of Jairus' daughter (Luke 8:41-42, 49-56)
Jesus Heals a Boy with Epilepsy (Luke 9:37-43)
Wedding at Cana (John 2:1-11)
Jesus Heals the Nobleman's Son (John 4:45-54)
The Lame at the Pool of Bethesda (John 5:1-18)
Feeding of the Five Thousand (John 6:1-14)
Jesus Walks on the Water (John 6:16-21)
Congenital Blindness Healed (John 9:1-41)
Healing of the Cripple at the Gate Beautiful (Acts 3; 4:4)

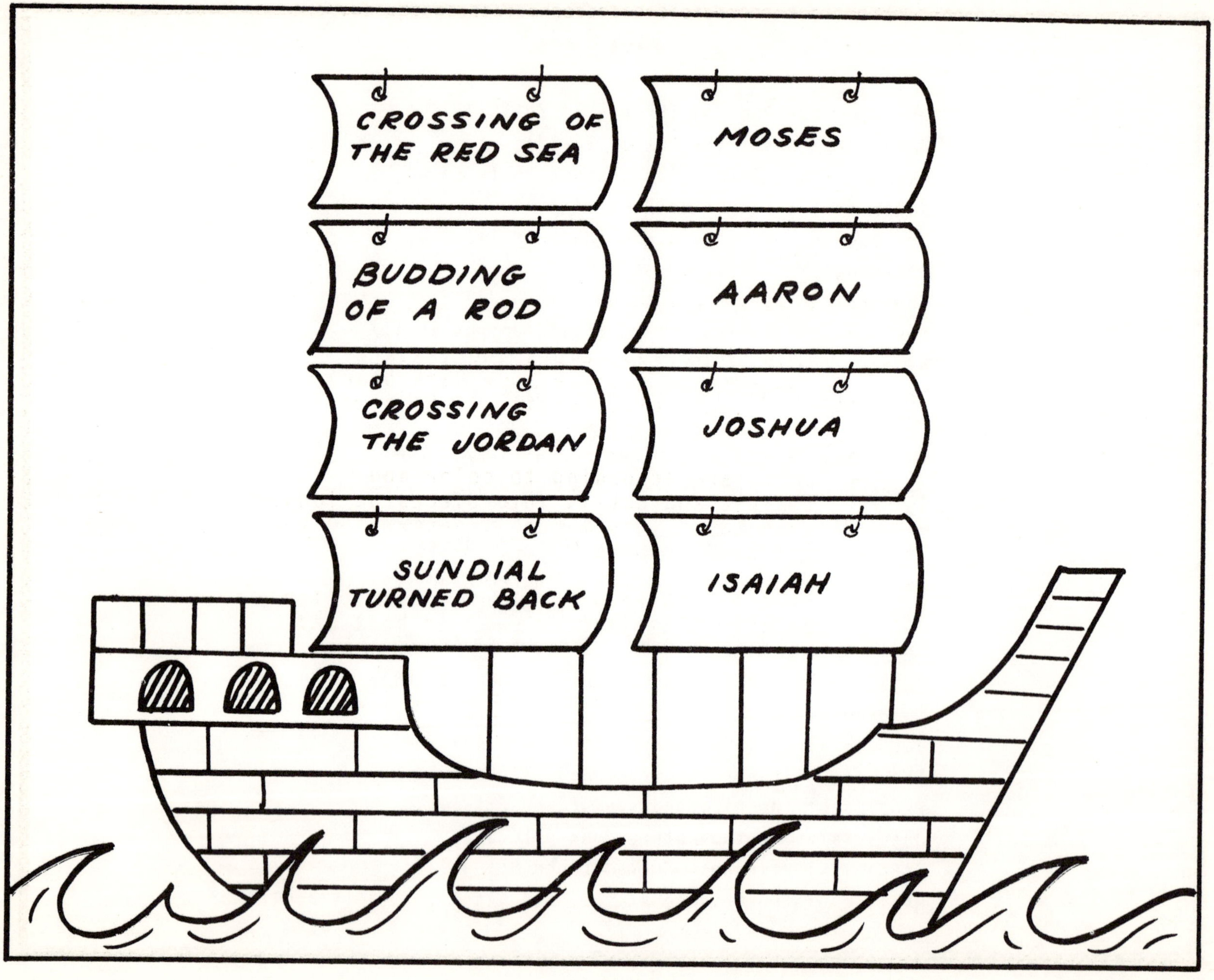
CROSSING OF THE RED SEA
MOSES
BUDDING OF A ROD
AARON
CROSSING THE JORDAN
JOSHUA
SUNDIAL TURNED BACK
ISAIAH

SUBJECT:	MIRACLES
ART ACTIVITY:	Yarn picture
MATERIALS:	Yarn in varied colors and textures (be sure to include some dark blue), glue, scissors, pencil, light blue construction paper
TEACHER PREPARATION:	Sort yarn according to color and texture and cut it into pieces no longer than 18". This makes it easier for the children to handle.
DIRECTIONS:	Sketch outline of boat on construction paper. Glue yarn to fill in boat and sea.

There are many miracles in the Bible. Each pair of pictures on this page tells the story of one of these miracles. Draw a line between the pictures that go together.

How many words with three or more letters can you make from the word MIRACLE? We found 30! Can you top that?

Cross out some of the letters in each group and you will find hidden words describing some of the miracles performed by Jesus. The letters are in the correct order and there is a pattern for each word.

Example: ~~S-O~~ M I ~~T-E~~ R A ~~M-O~~ C L ~~E-A~~ E S = MIRACLES

1. F O E I M E V T R E T R H A O R U M S T A L N C D F O R E M R D

____

2. O E L A S E T D P R I E C D R S C R L O E A A M N T S O E T D

____

3. T W A S L K M I N T G M O N M S W A W T E M R

____

4. T O E A M R P L E M S R T S W T R I L M L T E S D

____

5. A B L O I N T D C M A T N T C O U X R N E T D

____

SUBJECT:	THE CRUCIFIXION AND RESURRECTION
BIBLE REFERENCES:	Luke 23:33-24:53
LEARNING GAME:	The Last Supper
Materials:	Old gameboard or heavy cardboard, construction paper, felt pens, magnetic strips, scissors, glue
Construction:	Draw a large table. Cut loaves of bread from construction paper. Then cut the same number of goblets from construction paper. Write questions on the loaves of bread and corresponding answers on the goblets. Cut magnetic strips and place them on the table where the loaves and goblets are to be placed. Then place a piece of magnetic strip on the back of each of the loaves and each of the goblets. Answers may be written on the back of each cup.
DIRECTIONS FOR PLAYING:	The child matches the items by placing the goblet with its corresponding loaf of bread. The teacher should inform the students that the people whose names appear in this game took part in the last days of Jesus' life on earth, but they were not necessarily at the last supper with Jesus.

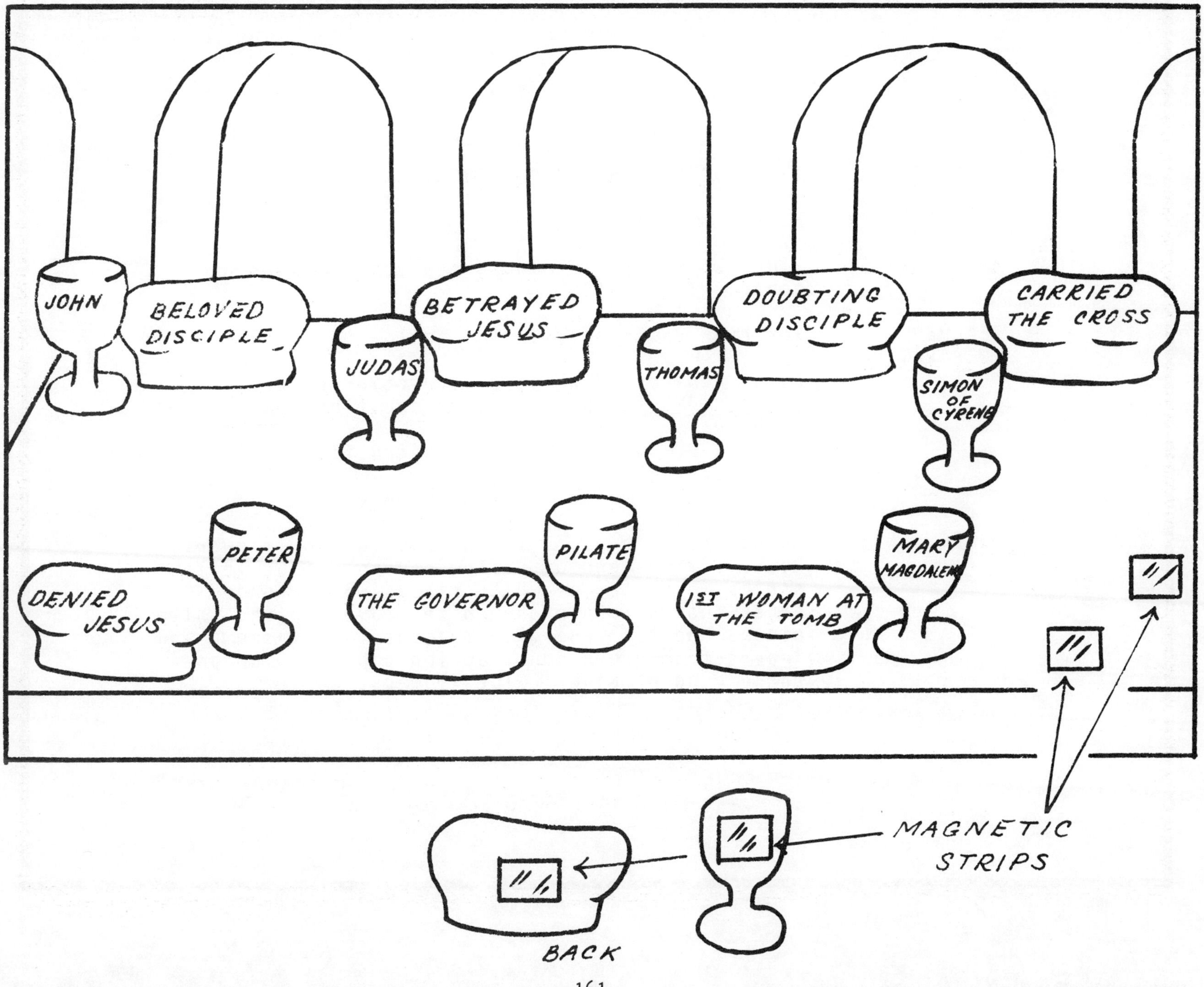
JOHN
BELOVED DISCIPLE
JUDAS
BETRAYED JESUS
THOMAS
DOUBTING DISCIPLE
SIMON OF CYRENE
CARRIED THE CROSS
PETER
DENIED JESUS
PILATE
THE GOVERNOR
MARY MAGDALENE
1ST WOMAN AT THE TOMB
MAGNETIC STRIPS
BACK

SUBJECT:	THE CRUCIFIXION AND RESURRECTION
ART ACTIVITY:	Easter lilies
MATERIALS:	Blue, white, yellow, and green construction paper, glue, scissors
TEACHER PREPARATION:	For each child provide the following: 2, 5" squares of white construction paper 2, 1" x 4½" strips of yellow construction paper 1, 3" x 9" strip of green construction paper 1, 9" x 12" blue construction paper
DIRECTIONS:	Round the corners of the 5" squares for flowers. Round off one end of yellow strips. Glue yellow strips in center of white pieces with rounded edges showing above the white. Overlap the white pieces about ¼" and glue together. Cut stems and leaves from green construction paper. Glue on background of blue. Glue flowers.

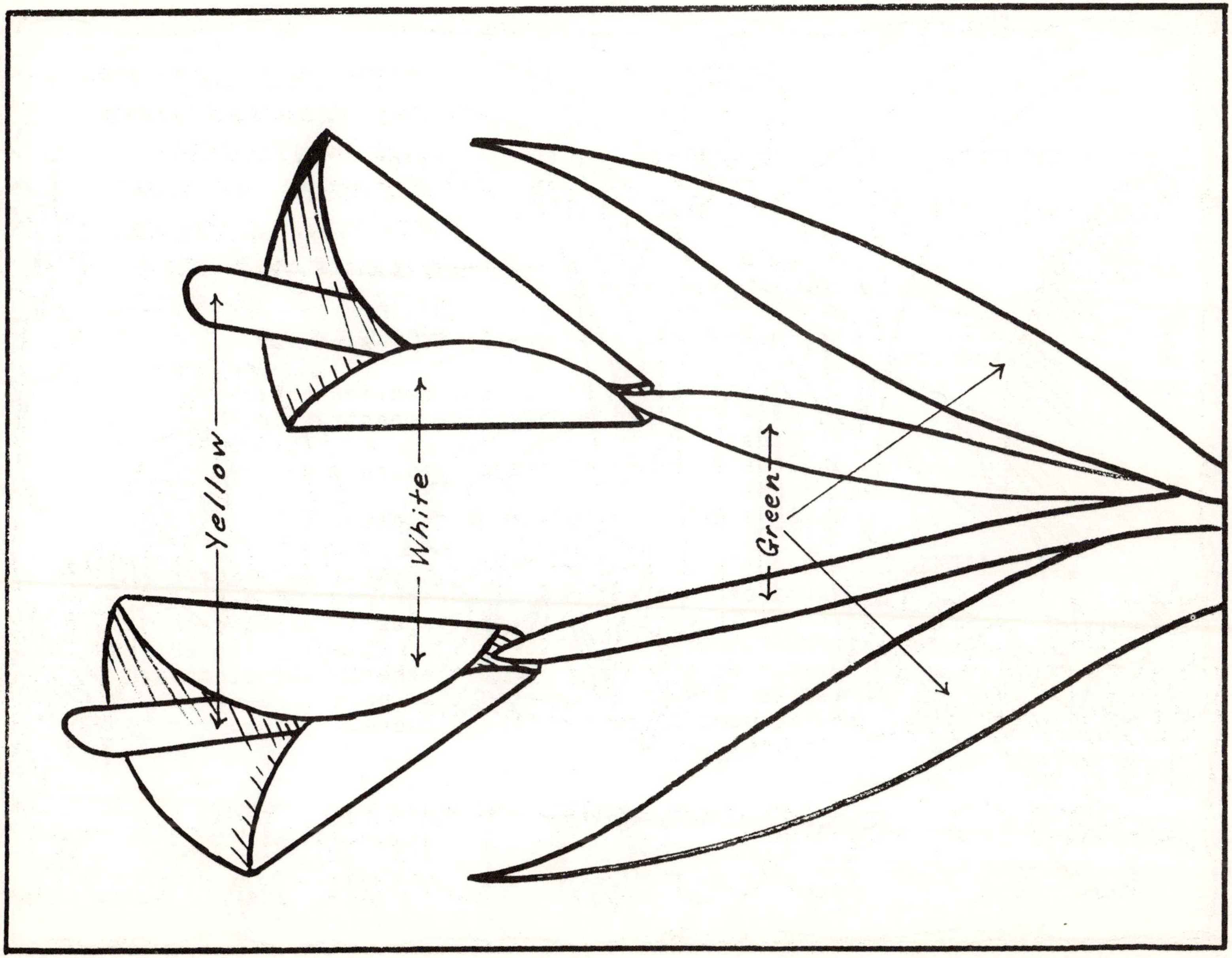
Yellow
White
Green

COPY THE LETTERS IN THE FLOWERS INTO THE MATCHING FLOWERS AT THE BOTTOM AND YOU WILL FIND THE ANGEL'S EASTER MESSAGE.
E
H
A
S
I
R
N

Beside each name write what each person is known for.

BARABBAS ______________________

PONTIUS PILATE ______________________

SIMON OF CYRENE ______________________

THOMAS ______________________

PETER ______________________

CAIAPHAS ______________________

JOSEPH OF ARIMATHEA ______________________

JOHN ______________________

JUDAS ISCARIOT ______________________

MARY MAGDALENE ______________________

Can you figure out the verse below with the help of the key?

Read it in Greek!

KEY

α = a	ν = n
κ = c	ο = o
δ = d	π = p
ε = e	ρ = r
φ = f	s = s
' = h	σ = s
ι = i	τ = t
λ = l	ω = w
μ = m	υ = y

'ε ιs νοτ 'ερε: φορ 'ε ιs

ρισεν, αs 'ε σαιδ. κομε,

σεε τ'ε πλακε ω'ερε τ'ε

λορδ λαυ.

__ __ ___ ____: ___ __

__ _____, __ __ ____.

____, ___ ___ _____

_____ ___ ____ ___.

SUBJECT: REVIEW

LEARNING GAME: The Bible Alphabet Train

Materials: Poster board, felt pens, construction paper, mystic tape

Construction: Cut poster board into three pieces: Two end pieces measuring 10½" x 9" and a center piece measuring 10½" x 10". Cut 20, 4" x 3-3/4" pieces of different colored construction paper for the cars. Fold each piece so it makes an envelope. Attach the three pieces of the board with mystic tape on front and back, making sure the 10½" x 10" is in the center. Cut an engine from black paper, and a caboose for "Z" from red paper. Cut 42 black wheels. Glue the engine on the top left of the poster board. Glue train cars and use mystic tape for the edges. Do not glue cars over folds on board. Glue wheels. Write the letters (see illustration) on the cars. Link each car to the other with a line as illustrated. Cut 21, 2½" x 2" cards. Write facts on each one, preferably close to the top of the card, so that when it is placed in the car, the fact can be read. Answers may be written on the back of the cards.

The following may be used for the cards:

A First man (Adam)
B Heathen god (Baal)

C First murderer (Cain)
D Killed a giant (David)
E Pharaoh's country (Egypt)
G Giant (Goliath)
H Samuel's mother (Hannah)
I Father nearly sacrificed him on mountain (Isaac)
J Led people after Moses died (Joshua)
K Herod (king)
L One of the Gospels (Luke)
M Moses' sister (Miriam)
N Built a big boat (Noah)
O King Ahab's governor (Obadiah)
P Jesus called him a "rock" (Peter)
Q They ate them in the wilderness (Quail)
R Joseph's mother (Rachel)
S Strong man (Samson)
U Bathsheba's husband (Uriah)
V Queen of Persia before Esther (Vashti)
Z A mountain in Jerusalem (Zion)

DIRECTIONS FOR PLAYING: The child matches each card to the letter and places it in the right car.

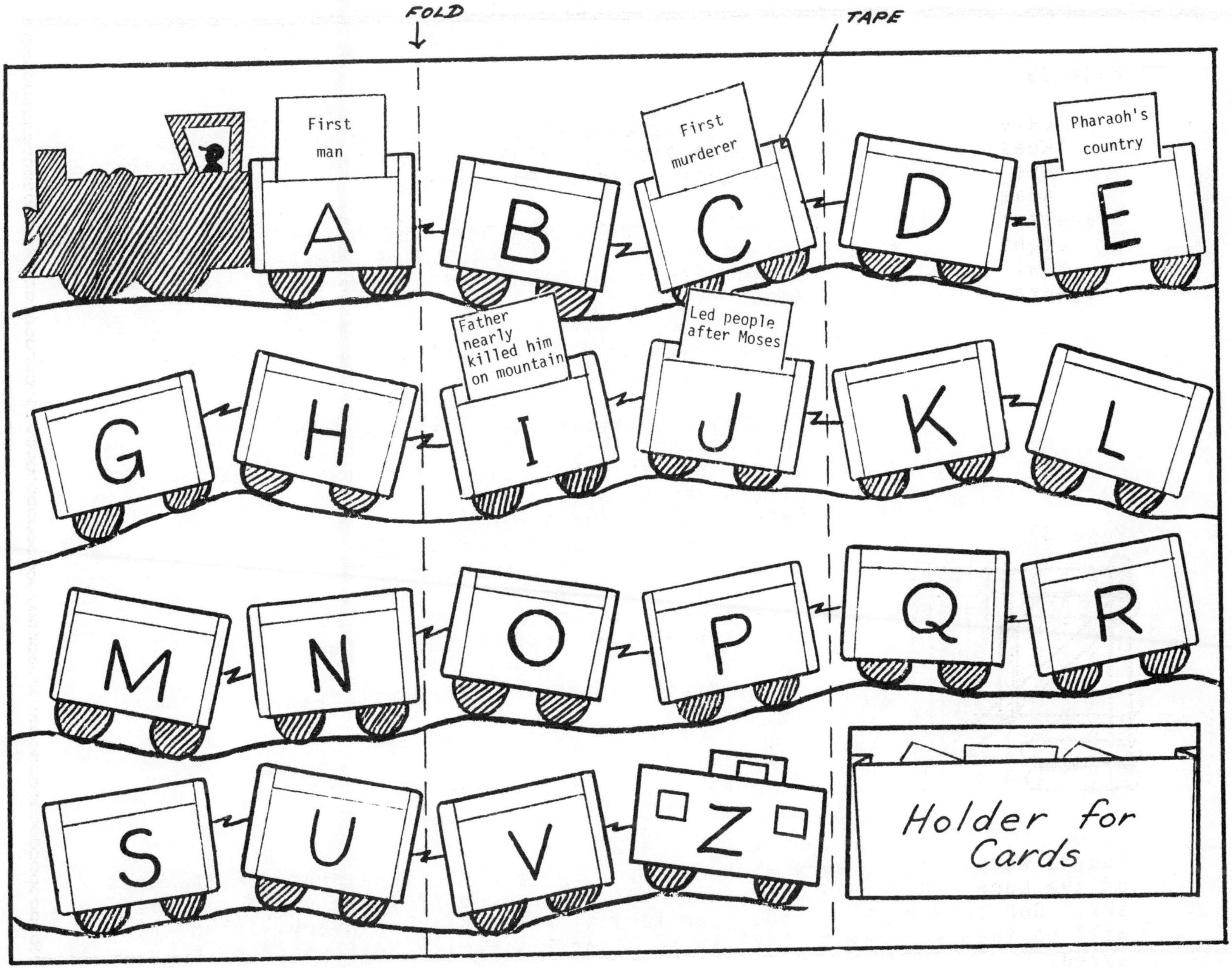
FOLD
TAPE
First man
A
B
First murderer
C
D
Pharaoh's country
E
G
H
Father nearly killed him on mountain
I
Led people after Moses
J
K
L
M
N
O
P
Q
R
S
U
V
Z
Holder for Cards

Page 29

Camel
TRees
Eve
Adam
PlaneTs
LIght
FOwl
SeveNth

Pages 30 and 31

In the beginning God made the world. God said, "Let there be light." He called the light Day, and the darkness Night. This was the first day.

On the second day, God made heaven.

On the third day, God made the grass, trees and flowers.

On the fourth day, He made the sun, moon, and stars.

Next God created the fish and birds.

On the sixth day, God said, "Let the earth bring forth living creatures." But God was lonely. And so God made man.

Page 37

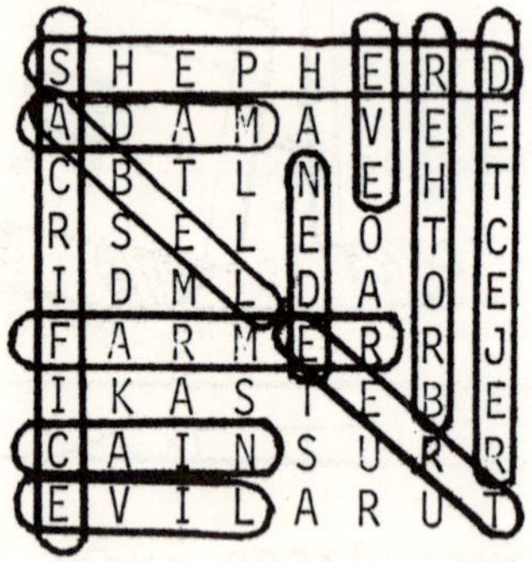

Page 38

1. This was the son of Cain.

2. Made Cain a vagabond and fugitive.

3. Cain did this to his brother.

Page 44

But Noah found grace in the eyes of the Lord.

Page 45

People were leading very wicked lives. Only Noah found grace in the eyes of the Lord. God told Noah about his plan to destroy the world. "Build an ark," God told Noah. "You, your family, and a pair of every living thing will go into the ark." Because Noah and his family believed God, they were saved.

Page 51

1. Sarah
2. Ishmael
3. Ur
4. Sodom
5. Moriah
6. House of God
7. Pharaoh
8. Pillar of salt
9. Eliezer
10. Melchizedek

Page 52

Abraham	kind
Babel	Lot
Canaan	Melchizedek
Desert	Nahor
Egypt	Offering
Fifty	Princess
Gomorrah	
Hagar	
Isaac	
Jordan	

Page 58

Ishmael
Potiphar
Daniel
Esau
dreamer
Laban
Esau
Abraham
Rachel
Benjamin

Page 59

1. Esau
2. Rebekah
3. Jacob
4. Laban
5. Bethel
6. Rachel
7. Leah
8. Benjamin
9. Israel
10. Isaac

Page 65

1. Jacob had given Joseph a coat of many colors.
2. One day Jacob sent Joseph in search of his brothers.
3. Joseph put on his colorful coat and began the journey.
4. When the brothers saw Joseph afar off they thought of a plot to get rid of him.
5. They threw him into a pit after stripping him of his coat of many colors.
6. After a while, some Arabs on camels passed by.
7. They were going to Egypt to sell slaves.
8. That gave the brothers an idea.
9. They lifted Joseph out of the pit and handed the Arabs twenty pieces of silver.
10. The brothers then took Joseph's coat and dipped it in the blood of an animal so that it would look as though a wild animal had attacked Joseph.

Page 66

Jacob loved Joseph the most out of his 12 sons. Because Jacob loved Joseph the most, the brothers were jealous.

One night Joseph had a dream. He told his brothers about it. It was about their sheaves bowing down to his sheaf.

Joseph had another dream. In this dream he saw the sun, moon, and

11 stars bowing down to him.

Jacob and his family lived at Hebron. Jacob's flocks were so large that there was not enough pasture nearby. One day Jacob sent his 10 sons to Shechem with the flocks. After some time Jacob sent Joseph in search of them.

When the brothers saw him, they tried to think of a plot to get rid of him.

Page 72

1.	Sinai	1.	Israel
2.	Tabernacle	2.	Zipporah
3.	Manna	3.	Pharaoh
4.	Canaan	4.	ram
5.	Nadab	5.	Raamses

Page 79

Amorites	Manasseh
Jericho	Jordan
Joshua	Moses
Israel	Caleb
Canaan	Achan

Answer: Commandments

Page 80

Moses	Jordan
Joshua	Israelites
Rahab	Canaan
Caleb	Achan
Jericho	Gibeon
	Shiloh

Page 73

Goshen: sprinkling blood on doorposts (Ex.9:26;12:23)
Midian: Moses worked there as a shepherd. (Ex.2:15;3:1)
Raamses: Israelites built the city. (Ex.1:11)
Marah: bitter water made sweet (Ex.15:23)
Elim: 12 wells of water (Ex.15:27)
Mt. Horeb: water from a rock (Ex.17:6)
Rephidim: Amalekites attacked (Ex.17:8)
Mt. Sinai: Ten commandments (Ex.19:18; 20)
Kadesh-Barnea: twelve spies sent out (Num. 13:26)
Mt. Nebo: Moses views the promised land. (Deut.34:1)
Mt. Hor: Death of Aaron (Num. 20:25-29)
Red Sea: Pharaoh's army drowned (Ex.14:23-28)
Hazeroth: Miriam smitten with leprosy (Num.12:10-16)

Page 86

1.	Nazarite	7.	Dagon
2.	Manoah	8.	Timnah
3.	judge	9.	lion
4.	hair	10.	honey
5.	Philistines		
6.	Delilah		

Page 87

1. Samson
2. Manoah
3. wife
4. Timnah
5. Philistines
6. Ashkelon
7. Ramath-lehi
8. Etam
9. hair
10. Gaza
11. Nazarite
12. Israel
13. offering

Answer: Samson's strong point was his strength.

Page 94

Eli
Samuel
Hannah
Dagon
Abinadab
Elkanah

Page 95

Hannah was childless so she asked God to send her a baby. God answered her prayer and sent her a son whom she named Samuel and dedicated to God. Samuel remained close to God throughout his life.

Page 103

1	2	3	4	5	6
add	awe	tamer	toe	ate	puppy
hat	are	fat	off	she	dusty
eve	toe	funny		set	cat
pie	ate	eye			ill
add	vet				mommy
					ask

Answer: David wrote many of the Psalms.

Page 104

Michal
Eleazar
Philistines
Hebron
Israelites
Baalim
Oil
Saul
Hushai
Ebenezer
Tabernacle
Heed

Page 112

1. False
2. False
3. False
4. True
5. True
6. False
7. True
8. True
9. True
10. False

Page 113

C	I	S	R	D	R	A	Y	E	N	I	V
H	N	A	B	O	T	H	U	R	X	Y	L
A	I	C	Z	R	S	T	V	I	W	E	Z
R	A	R	A	V	E	N	S	F	M	T	K
I	R	I	R	P	L	M	B	R	S	P	L
O	K	F	E	L	I	J	A	H	A	O	M
T	J	I	P	O	S	C	O	K	I	N	G
H	L	C	H	I	H	G	F	D	S	E	S
Z	A	E	A	Y	A	R	P	Y	R	E	K
M	A	W	T	L	F	W	K	V	A	U	C
A	B	A	H	A	E	H	O	T	E	Q	O
C	R	T	B	L	M	B	C	D	L	N	L
L	E	E	R	Z	E	J	E	R	I	M	L
O	B	A	D	I	A	H	V	W	E	H	U
Q	M	A	S	F	C	L	O	M	S	J	B

Page 120

1. The king liked Esther very much.
2. Esther saved her people.

Page 127

1. Shadrach, Meshach and Abednego
2. a little time
3. build a statue of himself and order all to worship it.

Page 135

Across:		Down	
1.	God	1.	Gourd
2.	Tarshish	4.	flee
3.	Nineveh	8.	city
4.	Fish	9.	ship
5.	prayed	10.	Jonah
6.	storm	11.	sea
7.	belly	12.	repent

Page 151

6. a. The Parable of the Ten Virgins teaches us to be spiritually ready.
   b. The Parable of the Sower describes the manner in which God's Word becomes effective.
   c. The Parable of the Prodigal Son is a story of God's forgiveness.
   d. The Parable of the Lost Coin pictures for us God's rejoicing over repenting sinners.
   e. The Parable of the Wedding Feast teaches that salvation is for all who accept it.

Page 121

Esther helped save the Jews.

Page 128

Daniel was thrown into the lions' den.

Page 142

Matthew 1:21: "And she shall bring forth a son, and thou shalt call his name Jesus: for He shall save His people from their sins."

Page 143

I bring you good tidings of great joy.

Page 157

Staff of Moses--snake
Water--rock
Multitude--loaves and fish
Aaron's rod--budding

Page 159

1. Five thousand fed
2. Leper cleansed
3. Walking on water
4. Tempest stilled
5. Blind man cured

Page 166

"He is not here: for He
is risen, as He said.
Come, see the place
where the Lord lay." (Matt. 28:6)

Page 158

lame	ram	clear	claim	meal	race
lace	mare	care	ream	rail	lime
calm	ace	arm	ear	era	air
alm	mail	are	clam	mire	aim
rim	car	came	lie	mile	male

Page 165

Barabbas: outlaw
Caiaphas: high priest
Joseph of Arimathea: tomb
Mary Magdalene: her hair
Pontius Pilate: Roman ruler
Peter: denied Jesus
John: beloved disciple
Judas Iscariot: betrayer
Simon of Cyrene: carried cross
Thomas: doubter

INDEX

ABRAHAM (Genesis 11:27–22:19) 46
BIRTH OF JESUS (Matthew 1:18–2:23; Luke 1:26–38; 2:1-20) 136
CAIN AND ABEL (Genesis 4) 32
CREATION (Genesis 1:1-2:14) 11
CRUCIFIXION AND RESURRECTION (Luke 23:33–24:53) 160
DANIEL (Daniel) 122
DAVID (1 Samuel 16:1–1 Kings 5:11). 96
ELIJAH (1 Kings 17:1–2 Kings 2:11) 105
ESTHER (Esther) 114
JACOB (Genesis 25:19–35:20) 53
JONAH (Jonah) 129
JOSEPH (Genesis 37:1–50:26) 60
JOSHUA (Joshua 1:1–24:30) 74
MIRACLES (See listing on page 153) 152
MOSES (Exodus 1:1–Deuteronomy 34:12) 67
NOAH (Genesis 6:1–9:27) 39
PARABLES (See listing on page 145) 144
SAMSON (Judges 13:1–16:31) 81
SAMUEL (1 Samuel 1:1–25:1) 89